UPSIDE DOWN

UPSIDE DOWN
DISCOVERING CREATION

WARD SMITH

Upside Down

Copyright © 2019 by Ward Smith. All rights reserved.

No part of this publication may be reproduced, stored in a retrieval system or transmitted in any way by any means, electronic, mechanical, photocopy, recording or otherwise without the prior permission of the author except as provided by USA copyright law.

The opinions expressed by the author are not necessarily those of URLink Print and Media.

1603 Capitol Ave., Suite 310 Cheyenne, Wyoming USA 82001
1-888-980-6523 | admin@urlinkpublishing.com

URLink Print and Media is committed to excellence in the publishing industry.

Book design copyright © 2019 by URLink Print and Media. All rights reserved.

Published in the United States of America
ISBN 978-1-64367-762-0 (Paperback)
ISBN 978-1-64367-761-3 (Digital)

25.07.19

CONTENTS

Acknowledgments 7
Prologue 9
Introduction 13

I: Diverse Paths to Belief 17
II: Naming 21
III: Occam's Razor 23
IV: Diversity 25
V: Information Flood 28
VI: Discovering Creation...31
VII: Finding God in Creation 34
VIII: Bible vs. Creation 41
IX: Searching for Balance 44
X: Separation 46
XI: The Creation Gap 48
XII: The Church 51
XIII: Our Competitive Edge 56
XIV: Church Identity Crisis 58
XV: Cognitive Dissonance 63
XVI: Complexity 67
XVII: So What 72
XVIII: God and Mind 76
XIX: God's Purpose 81
XX: Religion and Ethics 84

XXI:	The River	87
XXII:	Consciousness	89
XXIII:	Illusion and Reality	92
XXIV:	Science vs. Mind	98
XXV:	Lessons from String Theory	101
XXVI:	Religion	104
XXVII:	Paradox	112
XXVIII:	Free Will	114
XXIX:	Love	118
XXX:	The Way the World Works	121
XXXI:	The Struggle for Balance	124
XXXII:	Power Law	128
XXXIII:	Is Systems Theory Anti-God?	132
XXXIV:	Is Evolution Anti-God?	136
XXXV:	Religion is Small Potatoes	139
XXXVI:	Religion and Spirituality	143
XXXVII:	Philosophy vs. Religion	147
XXXVIII:	Transcendence	150
XXXIX:	A Better Way	155
XL:	Selling Passion	158
XLI:	Rescuing God	160
XLII:	The Bridegroom	164
XLIII:	Upside Down?	166

Epilogue: I don't live here anymore 169

ACKNOWLEDGMENTS

Again I thank Evelyn Shore for her enthusiastic support for this second work. I also thank Marcia Freeman and Audrey Pearston for their tireless editing and commentary.

PROLOGUE

Everyone has insights. Some people share; some do not. I have noticed that when someone is asked to give a supportive talk to a congregation about their own experience, they give a history. They do not share their personal belief. Perhaps they do not spend much time wrestling with religious belief. I have felt for some time that many people need a different way to think about their life and their religion. I am particularly concerned for the many traditional churches that have been losing members for decades. We'd like to think of it as a normal cyclical process, but after two or three generations we should suspect that something else is in play.

I have come to think of evolution as God's creation tool. This is not just about the evolution of man, but of all living and non-living things, about creation. I use a systems perspective in thinking about things. A complex living system is an organism acting as a whole whose stability is the result of webs of relationships. Living systems self-organize into stratified layers of systems and systems within systems. The human body is a typical example of such organization, as are social structures like family, community, government. Is it coincidence that Jesus felt that loving relationships superseded the Law and the prophets?

The primary requirement of living systems is survival. Living systems survive by efficient adaptation to their changing environment. As living systems adapt, they become more complex. As living systems, humans have increased in complexity to the level to exhibit mind. Systems Theory teaches that all living systems follow the same system rules and thus integrates all system activity whether individual, social, biological, medical, religious, corporate, or scientific.

We can think of Christianity as a sub-system in the greater system of religion. All religious systems are in relation to each other. Relationships may include resurrection, unconditional love, hierarchy, trinity, denomination, etc. Relationships may differ, but all are information pathways. Human systems, whether individual or corporate, evolve into identities that determine their response to information. All require efficient response to information, particularly disturbing information that heralds change to that system. Individual, group, church, government, or any living system that is ineffective in responding to change loses relevance in its changing environment.

This book offers the possibility for new insights by observing how the world and particularly the mind work as creations of God. His works might be treated as having equal status to his words, the Bible. His works, creation, and his words, the Bible, should be congruent. This might help to resolve the polarization and tension of naming: existence vs. non-existence; real vs. unreal; physical vs. non-physical; world vs. non-world.

The Bible describes man's inability to live within the laws of God, through many generations of his people. His chosen fail him. Being presented as controlling and vengeful, modeling man's behavior, has been ineffective. God then sent Jesus to model his message of loving relationships for mankind. Jesus challenged the past learning of his culture's identity. Obviously both God and Jesus were aware of the potential outcome. Man responded by killing Jesus in keeping with the behavior that had evolved to sustain human life in dangerous environments. Man was following his primary directive as a living system, as created by God. As a result of a diversity of positive and negative events in life, man is a mixed bag of positive and negative behavior. Man's self-defeating behavior has been expressed throughout biblical history and has continued to the present.

It is our nature to attempt to explain and communicate our ongoing experiences: our history. Without a system of writing, we used story-telling. The Noah story is thought to have been first written down about 900 B.C. The rest of the written Bible followed in bits and pieces: the Old Testament stories and then the letters and New Testament books. We have no knowledge of authorship. It seems to have been put together in pieces from many different sources. Finally, a committee evolved to assemble the Bible about 350A.D. This became the unifying document of the Christian religion, and with centuries of repetition became literal truth.

We are left with several insights:

- Evolution is God's creation tool, operating through diversity and adaptation.
- Our creative mind will make real for us (in the context of mind) any idea that we are willing to spend the time and effort to create, including a belief system.
- The nature of our learning system is such that it allows both self- enhancing and self-defeating behavior.
- The source of our learning is the environment into which we, without choice, are dropped.
- We are given rules and laws to live by, but we follow our own desire.
- Our reference is past learning, without consideration of the present or future.
- We respond to threats to this learning, our identity, with survival intent.
- Our survival intent, out of balance, suppresses God's intent.
- The church utilizes hell fire (control psychology) to give weight to God's intent and to its own authority, following system rules.

From a systems point of view, this is all natural, all created. So, how do we give God's intent power without resorting to a system survival response? It seems that we have to recognize human nature for what it is: human nature. The Biblical description of humanity that we are shot through with sin, that all of life is a struggle with cardinal sin is not helpful in sending a hopeful message for behavioral change. Self-defeating behavior is the result of years of repetition of thoughts about past negative experience. How do we break this chain? If through redemption, how and when are we truly contrite… when we are truly frightened of God's judgment… after we have passed through a series of church defined steps? We struggle with the self-defeating behavior that is an addictive artifact of our evolution.

It seems that Jesus is the source of motivation for change in this life. The Bible focuses on the requirements for life after death. We know that limiting or eliminating self-defeating behavior provides the opportunity for loving relationships. This is the way creation works. When is illogical self-defeating behavior forgivable and when is it unforgivable. When we say that we believe, does this mean that our behavior is acceptable? Or must our behavior, through loving relationships, validate our belief? Saying it does not necessarily constitute believing it. Is partial belief possible? If so, how much is enough? It is said that it is better to believe and be right than to not believe and be wrong. How does the created world respond to these questions? Logic would suggest that the word of God and the works of God should be congruent. Why do we continue to ignore the message of God's creation?

INTRODUCTION

Today's Christian worship is built primarily around the Bible as God's word, with major emphasis on the New Testament. Documents on both religious and historical analysis of the Bible would fill a library. Science, the analysis and measurement of God's creation, would fill another library. What seems to be missing is the analysis of God's creation from a religious point of view. What in the origin, systems, and process of creation support the insights in the religious and historical analysis of Bible. Our elevation of the Bible seems to have detracted from the religious awareness of God's creation to the point of invisibility, or at least irrelevance in the context of religion. Should we not expect God's creation, his works, to speak at least as loud as his words?

Since religion is primarily a belief system, we would expect that of particular interest would be religious consideration of human psychology and mind. An obvious area is the relevance of illogical, self-defeating behavior and its impact on building loving relationships, a foundational religious process. Another is the area of language and naming that impacts the sense of reality of religious thought. If these systems and processes are God's creation why do we create barriers that limit discussion between science and religion? Why can't we access the wealth of knowledge produced by scientific discovery in support of our religion?

Many scientists seem to have a consensus that there is no God in science or, if there is, God is most likely to be found in the sub-atomic, quantum world, not in the scientific world of Newton. On the one hand, we acknowledge that through faith we can agree that there is no evidence or logic to prove God's existence. On the other, we are always looking for proof and logic that God does or does not exist. We have come to awareness that all matter is illusion, in the sense that in the quantum world we find that all matter consists of patterns of energy and the space it occupies is mostly empty. We can say that matter is real in the context of Newtonian physics. In the quantum world, we are predicting patterns of energy so small that they are not measurable; therefore, they cannot be called science and thus are unreal.

The word context represents an environment in which naming takes on different meanings. We can say that God's creation (matter) is real in the context of Newtonian physics. In the quantum world of mathematics, we might say that some bosons, among the smallest particles theorized to date, are real in the context of the quantum math. They are not measurable, yet it seems that the universe could not exist without them. On this basis, we can take another step and say that ideas and mental constructs that exist in mind are real in the context of mind. We experience them, but cannot measure them. Without them humanity would not exist. This contextual use of the word 'reality' keeps the door open for discussion, allowing different kinds of reality. Labeling ideas as unreal does not increase our motivation to pursue them.

The long term trend showing a continuing reduction in church memberships in the First World has multiple causes. An obvious list comes to mind. However, we might also wonder whether there are systemic reasons that go beyond the obvious. We recognize a trend toward recreational churches. We recognize the increasing activity in our lifestyles and its impact on available time. We see the shift in priorities for using discretionary time. Are there opportunities that might reverse the membership trend? There are two systemic areas that might be candidates for consideration.

The first is best expressed with a passage from a child's story. In *Alice in Wonderland,* by Lewis Carol, Alice said to the White Queen that no matter how she tried she could not believe impossible things.

The White Queen responded, "Why some times I've believed as many as six impossible things before breakfast." The Church, like the White Queen, relies on preeminent status to support the authority of the *Bible* and its supporting biblical logic. Try as we may, there are some things that we just cannot believe. The resulting cognitive dissonance seeks redress.

The corollary to this passage is the sense of confirmation we get when we have the freedom to believe possible things. Evolution creates options for natural selection, for choice. This choice is based on ability to adapt, to fit into our changing environment. When we have choices and the freedom to choose, we choose what best fits our expectation. Perhaps the sense that evolution is congruent with freedom and choice is what causes us to believe that freedom and choice are instinctive, God given rights. Is a rigid hierarchal structure or an authoritarian structure a best fit for today's church?

A successful discipline requires acceptance of responsibility and pursuit of truth. Do we need better presentation of unbelievable scripture? Do we need more freedom and encouragement to participate in creating our individual belief? My sense is that unless we can increase that participation, we will have minimal ownership in belief and will continue to lose membership. We value what we work for. We value less what we have not worked for.

This book follows the style of my first book, *Who Me?*, as a series of essays that stream from one to the next. It utilizes the same lens of System Theory and Evolution to focus on the nature of God's creation, answering biblical elevation with the exclamation, "Me Too!"

CHAPTER I

DIVERSE PATHS TO BELIEF

Over biblical time and to the present, God has had many personas: Elohim, Creator, Lord, Master, JHWH, Wrathful God, Holy Spirit, Father, Son, Messiah, Teacher, Savior, Jehovah, Benevolent God, Friend. The many faces of our belief, all Christian, are diverse as is all of creation.

All believe that God has spoken to us through his Word, the Bible. At one end of our diversity, we have those believing that what God has said in the Bible, the written word, is infallible and in errantly true. Because of the large and growing quantity of evidence to the contrary, they support their belief based on the idea that any perception to the contrary is an illusion, a hoax played on the world by Satan, the deceiver. This belief engenders a passionate evangelical force directed at saving the world for God and from the evil clutches of Satan.

At the base of this fundamentalism is the idea that all humans throughout all generations are inherently evil, born into and hopelessly trapped in their sinful nature. In this evil world there is no possibility of escape. Life is a constant struggle against cardinal sin. The good news, the Gospel, is that Jesus through his sinless life and sacrifice has taken upon himself redemption of sin for all who believe in him. No human through any act can justify himself before God.

The only path is through Jesus. If not, he is lost, to be consumed in eternal fire. Because of the emphasis on salvation over repentance, baptism is held back until the member is deemed old enough to understand his choice to accept Jesus.

With salvation comes the obligation of repentance. While belief in Jesus brings salvation, salvation without repentance is false. Repentant acts signify proof of salvation and belief. We are what we do. What we believe is projected in what we do. They do not bring salvation. Repentance plays no part in salvation. Only Jesus can save. Fundamentalists accept that repentance is a continuous struggle that entails setbacks.

Many Christians seem as passionate in hating sin as they are in loving Jesus. Perhaps this is the same process. It is like a bad vs. good balancing act, a teeter totter. The further you bear down on sin, the higher you raise Jesus. If you are raising Jesus to the level of God, you must lower sin to the level of Satan. This becomes the life-long struggle with cardinal sin, a life long commitment to raise Jesus. Repentance is an individual process of strengthening belief. Salvation does not proffer the absence of sin.

At the opposite end of the Christianity spectrum are Christians that are committed to bringing religious dogma into the 21st Century. These Christians seek a world view that combines both science and religion. They make connections between religion and science (creation) in interpreting the Bible. This is not about changing the Bible, but rather changing insights to be inclusive, validating both the Bible and the way the world works.

If our belief is projected in our actions, then through our belief we are saved not through our actions. It is difficult to think about this without thinking about creation. That is, the way in which God created the working of the human mind. For the fundamentalist repentance comes after salvation. Many 'modern' Christians believe that they are born saved, beloved creations of God. Most believe baptism soon after birth marks them as Jesus' own. Belief is then the result of a learning process, the work of coming to believe. It is not justification for salvation, but rather a process for evolving of the mind to a level to accept what is already there, salvation. The way the mind works is that you become whatever you think about most. Your changing behavior may or may not count with God, but it is essential for a receptive change in your self. We learn through experience. We learn to accept and believe in Jesus. We learn to love ourselves to a level that allows us to project that love to our neighbors. We must make the mind a receptive place for Jesus to reside.

There are obviously many different ways to think about the process of coming to believe. For Christians, the objective is the same; it is acceptance and belief in Jesus. Jesus did not define who could believe and who could not. It is God's choice of evolution as the creation tool that provides the pattern of diversity and choice. People differ. Choices differ. What is unfortunate is that this diversity and the way the mind works can lead to illogical negative behavior: tyranny, territorialism, barriers, and fanaticism. Then, natural diversity, a creation of God, can become resistant to God's own purpose which is to create loving relationships. Jesus offers the path to fulfillment of God's purpose.

There are diverse paths to Jesus. Again, at one end is the path of fear and retribution. We and the world are evil and hopeless. We have no way to avoid our condition. The wages of this condition are eternal hell fire. Salvation comes only through accepting and believing in Jesus. At the other end is the path of love. We are God's beloved creation. The creation process results in both positive and negative attributes that we project in our behavior. Negative behavior can be perceived as sin and at some level evil. Negative attributes of our being are resistant to God's purpose. We must do the work of limiting or eliminating negative behavior to become aware of and receptive to God's love. Again, Jesus offers the path to fulfill God's purpose. If the mind creates whatever we think about most, what will each process, fear or love, deliver? God's message through the Bible was written down in a very dangerous world where fear and retribution were survival behaviors. This behavior is still dominant, but is changing toward a more benevolent culture. It is interesting to see the change in the names of God as ideas about belief change through the centuries, moving from distant to wrathful to benevolent. Christianity is a force for this positive cultural change.

Knowledge is growing in the modern world that fear and retribution are in opposition to the way the mind works in accomplishing God's purpose. This survival behavior in the modern world of technology is threatening survival. We now talk about the possibility of extinction events created by misuse of technology. Given Man's penchant for survival behavior, is it better to flood the mind with thoughts of fear, or with thoughts of love? It is natural that between the opposing ideas of fear and of love are many variations that combine both ideas. All are Christian ideas seeking salvation through Jesus. God's message is integration through the acceptance of his diversity, not separation. Separation limits or eliminates loving relationships.

God's creation, our universe, has perhaps forty quadrillion stars, in 170 billion galaxies. Our biblical logic supports the idea that we are the central characters on this cosmic stage. Our presence in a practical sense is equivalent to a grain of sand on a beach. Yet, there is one astounding fact that might forgive our arrogance. We are complex living systems that have evolved to the level to exhibit mind. We contain the most complex living system in the known universe, the human brain. Our brain has one hundred billion neurons, and as many synapses as there are stars in the universe. Imagine looking up into the brain as we might look up into night sky, and imagine that each synapse is a light source. We then find ourselves looking at the universe of Mind, a universe God copied from the original and tailored to fit the human skull. We are God's star children, his beloved creation. Let this be the beginning of our journey toward belief.

CHAPTER II

NAMING

My name is Ward Smith. This is what I am called, not who I am. I am also known by a social security number. This implies that I have certain legal rights under the laws of the United States, but it is still not who I am. I am a unique entity in genus Homo and species sapiens. While I am a physical entity, diverse in the ways of Nature, who I am is best expressed by an as yet non-definable, non-physical construct of mind. I have my being in the most complex living system in the universe, the human brain. I project who I am in my behavior, making my non-physical being a physical reality. The sum of all this is my personality, or my unique identity. I imagine that it could take a lifetime to exhaust the possibilities associated with naming.

In the dim past, in order to get some order in the chaos of the infinite possibilities of our identity, we became aware of "God". It became obvious very early in human thought that naming God would add another layer of chaos to a world already too complex to comprehend. To personify God, God was given a name, or several names, in keeping with the diversity of Nature. Now, as God has a name or names, we are drawn into the same problem. Well, who or what is God? We can't really answer that for ourselves, let alone for God. We are left to struggle with defining the non-definable… chaos again. Who is God? What our creative mind cannot understand, it creates for us to soothe our anxiety. We will continue the struggle to define the non-definable. Curiosity and creativity cannot be denied.

We are still chasing the Mathematics for Unified Field Theory, the holy grail of physicists. With this we will be able to provide a logic that fits the dynamic forces from planets to bosons, the smallest known particles in our quantum world. We are aware that the entire universe is in a dynamic dance of energy, with its own quantum rules. Perhaps it is this superstring substance that we are describing mathematically that is the dirt of the universe.

Perhaps God used this dirt in creating the universe, just as the dirt of the earth is said to have been used to create Adam. We might assume that the dirt of the earth and the quantum dirt of the universe are one in substance. It is the evolutionary process: create, select, and adapt, that has carried us from bosons to the human brain and mind. Name it Big Bang, or Inflationary Expansion, our world exists. We will soon have a name for the dirt of the universe, super strings, or perhaps super-super strings as we add more mathematical strands to each vibrating string, allowing us to straddle both the quantum and Newtonian physical worlds. Will that name be an identifier, or will it be what it really is… another way to describe chaos, a universe of dancing patterns of energy?

CHAPTER III

OCCAM'S RAZOR

It is not difficult to understand that the teachings of the New Testament regarding one's neighbors are a recipe for peace and good mental health. Because it is couched in religious doctrine, many people 'throw the baby out with the bath water'. I have come to understand that it is O.K. to not understand that which cannot be understood. Why should I deny something because it is something that I can't prove? It is interesting to think of science as built on the defining of theories about that sort of thing. At least, theories last until they can be disproved.

I believe that it is important to maintain an attitude of curiosity about religion. In this process, I try to understand how science as we know it, and nature, as we experience it, support the teachings of Jesus. This is not the same thing as trying to prove the existence of God. It helps me to understand how some people attempt to validate their belief in the non-existence of God. My conclusion is that many people are not really rejecting God, but rather are rejecting their past experience of God. Many of our irrational behaviors are built on a foundation of unhealthy childhood experiences (shifting sand?).

I think about how the world works. I find in the various ideas about life such as Systems Theory, Catastrophe Theory, Evolution, Psychiatry, Psychology, etc., both a complexity and an evolving unity that is meaningful to me. I interpret the Bible as the story of man's struggle that evolves through the trials and errors of people through out the Old and New Testament. I find consistency in my understanding of evolution and its resulting diversity as the primary tool for man's progress. I have no trouble with a 'God' entity's use of this tool to develop and nudge mankind toward a Godly purpose.

While I find "Father" as a practical way to give a sense of substance to a spiritual being, I find God as The Holy Spirit more consistent with the current understanding that all matter is made up of patterns of energy (activity). That might present "God" as The Sentient Pattern of Energy, or The Holy Spirit. The problem with using 'Father' for the name of God is that today many unfortunate people do not have a healthy remembrance of their father. This makes it difficult for them to have an open mind when considering the existence of God. On the other hand, how do we gain a sense of personal relationship with an entity named 'Holy Spirit'?

As Episcopalians, we have a lot of flexibility in our freedom to think about the nature of God and The *Bible*. To get bound up in (be obsessive about) trying to understand the nature of "God" or in making biblical wording rigid is pointless. To try to understand that which is not understandable is a zero sum game. I find it easier to just believe. Call it Occam's razor (the simplest alternative is likely to be the correct alternative). This brings us back to what 2000 years of Christian religion has prescribed, "Blessed are those who have not seen and yet believe."

What I believe is most meaningful is to gain the understanding that we are all deficient in some way or another. We cannot justly judge others without reflecting on our own brokenness. Our individual skills in creating a safe (welcoming, non-judging) place for our neighbors and ourselves are essential for a more abundant life. Perfecting these skills should be our life's work of love.

CHAPTER IV

DIVERSITY

Evolution is nature's primary process for change. It is through this process that all living systems have been created. Diversity is a fundamental property of evolution. Diversity is the canvas on which evolution paints nature's living landscape. Diversity covers both the physical aspects of life and the dynamic processes by which living systems prevail.

In discussions about "the way the world works" we lift ourselves above the living world to view the living forest, while acknowledging that active agents, trees, are living systems within the greater living system, the forest. We are a living system in a layered structure of systems within systems: individual, family, community, state, country, or member, parish, diocese, ECUSA, Anglican Convention. We are all systems within systems, having interdependencies within ourselves, with our associated systems and within the environment in which we are imbedded. We emphasize that it is the relationships between these layers that support their stability, allowing them to grow. The total is greater than the sum of the parts. That which is greater than the sum of our physical body and self-awareness is awareness of others. Relationships are self-transcending.

Diversity is often shown as a Gaussian distribution plot, the range of a behavioral attribute extending from one extreme to the opposite extreme. Given behavior as a mix of both good and bad behaviors, we would have people with all good behavior at one end and people with all bad behavior at the opposite end of the plot. The resultant bell shape has most of the people, with a mix of both good and bad behavior in or near the center of the plot.

The problem with diversity in mental attributes that project behavior is the work required to maintain a practical or comfortable balance between opposing ideas. It takes less energy to be all one thing or all its opposite than to struggle for balance. There are two responses in opposition to diversity. One is the idea of equality and the other is certainty. As Christians we are apt to think that distribution of wealth, or standard of living, should be equal for everyone. Unfortunately, population growth always exceeds growth in wealth. Attempts to obtain equal distribution results in actions that destroy the system for creation of wealth. These attempts equate to a history of collapse, dictatorship and eventual rebirth.

Certainty can be seen as the extreme at either end of a behavioral attribute. Certainty results in polarization of any behavioral distribution. The normal or central tendency is always a mixed bag. Certainty has the quality of closure. Its truth is unassailable and makes dialogue impossible. It also appears to convey the right and obligation to impose that truth on all related groups. While certainty implies closure, its obligation to project that truth makes the work of protecting its territory energy intensive. We can see this in operation in the U.S. Congress. Both Parties have an extreme element (far right and far left) that has made dialogue impossible. We see the same process in religion regarding biblical interpretation.

It is evident that opposition to diversity is an action that challenges freedom and choice. It is the territory of control psychology. Given this orientation, it is clear that such behavior is typical of theocracies and dictatorships. It is also the reason for the cyclical failure of democracies. Democracies are based on dialogue and the negotiation of issues of the major system by its sub-systems. Polarization of a system is symptomatic of system failure. It is predictable that subsystems will tend to support their own survival and growth at the expense of the greater system. At some point, this process becomes irreversible. It is the diversity of ideas and the ability of a system to act efficiently on those ideas, even when they herald significant change that represents a healthy system. The aging process is one of hardening and of clogging the information pathways that are the webs of relationships that stabilize any system.

The natural process, evolution, supported by diversity, is the way the world works. Diversity provides the options for natural selection in the process of evolution. If evolution and diversity are God's creation tools, why do we still, with tribal behavior, denigrate differences at the expense of greater understanding that the survival of living systems is dependent on an abundance of differences? Thank God for creating diversity.

CHAPTER V

INFORMATION FLOOD

When I spoke of the information flood in a meeting, a participant said that he did not believe that there was an information flood. He spoke of experiences as a child when hiking with his uncle who had an amazing knowledge of all sorts of plants and animals. He felt that every generation experiences being flooded with information. There is a difference in knowing or being aware of things because we have experienced them. Some of us experience more than others. Some of us have a curiosity that pulls us into new experience. It is natural for most people to feel secure in their past learning. It's who they are and they avoid change as unnecessarily painful.

The information flood that I refer to is the information that is too voluminous to experience. We humans have limits to how much experience we can handle and to the rate at which it impacts us. We are at the end of the telecommunication funnel, overwhelmed with both the quantity and the velocity of incoming information. This is not just an individual problem, but a cultural problem. This is a technology driven phenomenon, devouring information and expanding in step with the new information it makes available. This telecommunication phenomenon is coupled with a parallel applications technology phenomenon necessary to access and use the flood of information. Information sources have gone from local to global while cultures that vary from primitive to modern are relatively static. Robotics and electronic classrooms are changing the nature of work. Communication is personal and instant through the Internet, with equipment changing every 2-3 years. How do we deal with this?

The answer appears to lie in specialization, segmentation. It is about cutting it into digestible amounts. Specialization has been common in areas such as medicine with a triage model of doctors of internal medicine directing the flow of patients to various specialists after a variety of diagnostic procedures. The types of engineers and scientists are constantly expanding. This fractioning of professions is filtering down into colleges and high schools who struggle to keep up with the changing job market. All of this is impacting our various cultures that are forced to keep up. The specialization is creating new sub-languages, creating territorial boundaries which impact understanding. This has long been a problem between scientists and engineers who tackle problems from opposite ends. It is little wonder that we admire those so-called renaissance personalities who can span multiple knowledge areas.

We are faced with the realization that the human mind treats information as its food. It ingests, digests, and assimilates the information and then creates new information. The information flood puts pressure on mind to increase this cycle that, in turn, feeds back on its self. The mechanism of mind is brain. The physical brain has a very slow evolutionary rate of change. The mind has a very rapid evolutionary rate of change. We know that the brain is highly energy consuming. We know that if we overwork the brain, we experience the result as exhaustion and headache. We also know that exhaustion and headache are largely associated with our inability to maintain our identity in the face of new information.

Those who love learning have a much higher pain threshold for learning. We see individuals with incredible capacity to take in information and individuals who have incredible capacity to create new ideas. The one does not necessarily go with the other. The brain has different pathways. We also see that very high IQs tend to relate with social dysfunction. This is likely more to do with our culture's incapacity to accommodate genius. A genius is not particularly useful in many situations where his or her self-esteem is such that they have trouble sharing in teams.

When dealing with complex living systems, individual or group, how do we accommodate when change is inhibited by rigid expectations and perceptions, and their projected behavior? Pacifists do not tackle the major problems of our society with the intent of change. The motivation of anger, survival behavior, is required; i.e., as if your life depended on it. We are again challenged to find a practical and motivational balance between anger and compassion. Major social problems cannot be handled alone. It requires large groups of people creating pressure for change.

The more pain we feel, the greater will be our motivation to change. The problem is systemic. If we can't find the escape hatch, we become indifferent and then hopeless. If there is no specific source to address, then broad and sweeping blaming begins with resultant revolution and anarchy. It then takes a dictatorial power and lethal force to gain control. This is the history of democracies. All of this is not the result of intent, but the unwillingness to take responsibility at a time when correct action might alter the pattern. It is the result of indifference among the greater population. This is the rich earth of illogical, self-defeating, survival behavior. There will always be a few individuals that believe in their right to control by defining truth for the masses.

CHAPTER VI

Discovering Creation

It was a beautiful autumn day. My friend and I were tending the lawn at our church, St. Chrysostom, where God's bounty includes an endless supply of leaves. I had been admiring the dazzling color display and a thought popped into my head. I asked my friend, what is a *Bible*? He said a book. Ok what else… a religious book? Ok what else… the word of God. I thought yes, the Bible has been presented as the word of God for 17 centuries.

I then asked him to look around. What do you see? The church, what else? The trees, what else? Houses, what else? He asked where I was going with this. I asked, do you believe in God? He said, yes, of course. Do you believe he is the creator? He said yes. Then, I asked, what are you seeing? He did not respond. I said, "You are looking at creation". You, yourself, are the created. If we perceive the *Bible* as the words of God, why do we not perceive the created as the works of God? For 17 centuries we have held the *Bible* up as the word of God, and allowed God's creation, his work, to become invisible, at least irrelevant, and at best, a gift to be thankful for. Where is the religious awe? Where is the analysis to find God's creation message for us? We commonly say that acts speak louder than words. Eastern mystics seem to have heard the message: All is one. All is connected. God's message is integration, not separation.

By the 16th Century, the Church had so much dogma based on biblical logic that stating a fact in opposition was a capital offense. In spite of the resulting schism that created many variations in Christian worship, the *Bible* remained the word of God. Today this is not questioned. While many churches understand stories to be stories and treat some passages as metaphorical, there are still many believing in the inerrancy of the *Bible*. Science and technology in the past hundred years has discovered much of the way our created world works, and created technologies for archeology and document analysis that challenge biblical inerrancy. This does not challenge the value of the *Bible*, or its status as a bearer of God's message. It does reflect on the human interpretation of God's message.

The 16th Century brought the idea that science should be separated from philosophy, religion, and medicine because they could not be measured. This strategy has resulted in an incredible blooming of science. Religion began to bloom when loss of Church control in that period brought freedom of thought though religious intolerance has followed us to this day. For controlling personalities, the opportunity to control religious belief is an intoxicating attractant.

Imagine how difficult it is to take a population of people and over time evolve a unified culture. History has shown that the bloody struggles involved in such a process are required in the creation of unifying documents. The *Magna Charta* is an example. Our **Constitution** is an example. The *Koran* is an example. The *Bible* is an example. The *Bible* combines both the history of the struggle and the resulting document or documents. For these unifying documents, the theme is to make the document time and culture independent so that it becomes a lasting truth and guide. But, history evolves. Cultures evolve. Environments evolve. We study both the unifying documents and their historical origin to find the insights that have made such documents universal and timeless.

There is always pressure for change. The *Bible* is our oldest unifying document and has changed little in nearly 2000 years. The struggle with interpretation has turned unity into multiplicity, into a diversity of separate groups, each with their preferred insight. Religious tolerance is a fragile thing. The *Koran* suffers the same diversity, following the same bloody path that mirrors the past of Christianity. We are left to realize that our great unifying ideas evolve from our hope for freedom and a safe way of being, but humanity to date continues to project the behavior of its evolutionary struggle for survival. We preach unity while building boundaries and following win/lose strategies.

The human condition today is that science is left to study and make discoveries about God's creation, while the churches struggle to find the relevance of creation by studying the *Bible*. Scientists generally find in their research whatever their expectations and perceptions direct them to, evidence of God and evidence of no God. System Theory suggests that most likely it will be new churches that will utilize the discoveries of science and the creations of technology to adapt Jesus' message to our new and changing environments. We can expect them to be multiple and cultish in their embryonic passion for life.

CHAPTER VII

FINDING GOD IN CREATION

Faith is the proposition that there are truths that cannot be proven by logic or evidence. This does not insure that God exists. It gives us justification for our belief in the existence of God and our searching for God's purpose. We find the history of man's struggle to find God in the Old and New Testament and in many myths and religions that predate the monotheism of our Jewish roots. Over half of the population of earth believes in the God of Judaism, the God of Christianity and the God of Islam, the one God.

We arrive in God's creation without any awareness of the what, where, how or why of our existence. We begin the journey of mental development in the womb, learning at a phenomenal rate, making synaptic connections at thousands per second. Whether we get to believe in God, or not is perhaps one chance in two. Our life journey is not a predictable process, nor is it an equal opportunity one. What we learn is that ideas to which we are exposed, the events in our lives, have the most enduring imprint when we are children.

Cradle Christians who fed our adult church membership in the past are becoming increasingly scarce as church membership dwindles. Learning to believe is a mental process involving many of creation's systems and processes. One way to learn is in repetition of the lessons and stories of the Bible. Another is to ask questions about and study the systems and processes that allow us to learn and to come to believe. We are constantly learning new things about the history of our origin and the way we have evolved. We see this as an ongoing process requiring continuing change and adaption to change. As a result, we are continuously developing new insights and ways of thinking about our existence and our beliefs.

We know very little about the God, Elohim, who created the universe from beyond the cosmos. All we know is that his actions were magical and beyond the chemistry and physics of today's world. We know also that his creations were pronounced good. This was a distant God. The God that created Adam and Eve was a 'hands on' God who used the dirt of the earth to create Adam, and presumably all the plants and animals of Adam's time. He was also a vocal God who spoke with Adam and Eve, with Noah, a number of others over time and finally about his son, Jesus, at Jesus' baptism. In return for obedience, God promised to provide the means and opportunity for his people to multiply. From the biblical God's view, it has been a bumpy road. Man has had a similar view.

Among all the dos and don'ts, a clear message comes out of both the Old and New Testament that loving one's neighbor as one's self is like unto the admonition to love God. Since Jesus repeated this insight 2000 years ago, our history suggests that it is contrary to human nature. History also shows that it is the most popular insight in history. We just can't seem to do it. Still, it haunts us like the song of unconditional love that introduced us into this created world. It is likely that the answer to this conundrum lies in God's creation, not in his word. While we place his word, the Bible, high in our esteem, we seem to forget our world is his creation, his work.

Most people today don't believe that God just zapped the world into existence. There is too much factual evidence to the contrary. That being the case, we must look for answers in God's creation, not in or not just in the Bible. We imagine God as a benevolent father figure. We seem to stop there. We don't imagine that God had to make a decision just how he would accomplish the making of the universe. What were his options? What were his tools? Our studies of his creation, Science, indicate that he used Nature's systems and processes, God's systems and processes. We call them physics and chemistry. We call them evolution, systems theory, complexity theory, chaos theory, mathematics, etc. etc. We have come to know a great deal about the physical aspects of God's creation.

It is unfortunate that we have come to define the evidence of science as real and the ideas of religion as unreal. This seems to prevent us from looking for confirmation of biblical insights in God's creation. The elevation of the Bible as God's word has eclipsed the possibility of religious study of God's creation. The idea that we are descended from apes has served to reject the idea of evolution. This naïve simplicity required 80 years to overcome. Evolution was finally accepted in the 1930s. Actually, chimps are more likely ancestors with 97% of our same genetic makeup. We now know that DNA is the thread that binds all living things. The code is universal in living organisms, plant or animal, microbe or man. The message of DNA is that all are one.

The diversity of nature is a result of evolution, driven by life's God given instinct for survival. The incredible number of improbable events that have marked our evolutionary path to this point is beyond counting. Genetic mutation is slow to the point of stasis. All life began as molecules growing in complexity. A big step was the evolution of a cell wall that turned a drop of liquid into an entity. A cell was a bag of liquid until one cell tried to engulf and digest another cell. It was found indigestible and more useful as a nucleus than as food.

With the nucleus, cells had the capacity to create new and useful protein molecules, using DNA, increasing their complexity. Then a cell reached the level of asexual reproduction, replicating themselves in a manner of minutes. Then cells found advantage in sticking together. The stage was set for larger organisms… and so on and so on. Interestingly, 80% of the mass of living systems on earth is microbial, in a thousand varieties. They seem to fit any environment that nature provides, with minimal change and naturally selected.

Extinction events that killed off macro-life could not seem to touch micro-life.

Evolution's magic is in its random branching that shortens evolution's time scale. The larger and more complex life becomes, the more difficult it is to adapt to rapidly changing environments. Large animals require abundant food. Their size and design makes them invincible. The dinosaurs survived hundreds of millions of years until an epic natural phenomenon took away their food and water. Only animals the size and burrowing nature of rodents survived, fortunately including mammals. Epic changes in environment due to volcanoes, meteorite strikes and tectonic upheavals which change weather patterns have allowed this random branching. Evolution is not a continuous monolithic process. It seems to occasionally erase and rethink its path. There are no guarantees. These major extinction events (about 6 to date) suggest that there may be a limit to our time on the evolutionary stage to complete our act in God's play.

Most of the earth's rocks are sub-ducted back below the earth's surface due to the action of the earth's tectonic plates. The oldest known rocks are about 4.3 billion years old. Rocks found containing evidence of early life are about 3.8 billion years old. This suggests that life began when the earth was still a hot and volcanic environment. The message of creation seems to be that life was and is a very important part of the creation story. Does this imply intent… a God purpose? Most of us unconsciously shape our lives to fit our expectations. Most people think it does.

Early Man, hominids, began to show up in the fossil record around 1.7 million years ago. Early hominids left the trees to become dwellers of the savannahs, evolving into Homo erectus. This was probably due to the blocking of the passage between North and South America which changed weather patterns and caused the beginning of the desertification of Africa. Homo erectus evolved into Homo sapiens. About 100,000 years ago, likely due to continued desertification, Homo sapiens migrated out of Africa. Thus, Man began the population of Europe and Asia. All of the current races of Man have their roots in Africa. Life challenges us to survive. Again the creation message is: All are one; survive.

More than anything else, the last 100,000 years of creation has been about survival. Eighty percent or more of that time has been about discovering how to make fire and tools and obtain food. Another 15% was about learning to socialize, to live in groups for protection and to work in groups to more efficiently supply food. Again, life was about survival. The last 5000 years have been about dynasties. The emphasis has been on large groups and large territories, rather than individuals. Beginning in this time period, the idea of gods that control all of Nature became popular as a way of dealing with the fear of the unknown and of offering hope for individual and group survival. Religions became as powerful as governments in seeking control of the populous and establishing themselves as national religions. This bureaucratic behavior of groups continues to the present day, a group example of survival behavior: grow or die.

In the last 100 years, we have begun to understand the working of the most complex of God's living systems, the human brain, and Mind. We know that the opposing sensations of pleasure and fear are our most basic motivations. We realize that an excess of either damages ourselves and others. We are hard wired for anger to give us the strength and agility for physical struggle. Our learning system utilizes pleasure to overcome the stress associated with learning new information that counters our past learning. Our reproductive system uses pleasure to insure procreation. We know that what is good can also be bad. There are limits that keep us within an emotional range for self- enhancing behavior. We are evolved for a healthy life. We have the mental freedom to choose to stay within limits or not to. Religion functions to pressure us to stay within a 'normal' range of behavior.

We have evolved to establish a strong identity and to respond to challenges to that identity as though our lives depend on it. Our behavior is the evolutionary result of a history that required such a response for survival. As our environment has evolved to be more sociable and to define rules for proper behavior, the need for survival behavior has become less of a requirement. Hopefully, our culture is changing toward a more compassionate and empathetic society. What were essential behaviors for survival are no longer routinely necessary.

Our survival nature is strong and its pace of change is not necessarily consistent with the pace of our changing ideas. We are a long way from a time when our culture will be one of predominantly loving neighbors. We hear about the idea and see rare examples of such a nature, but more prominent are the self-serving individuals and groups who operate with an excessively controlling nature. This is a constant reminder that slows our evolution toward a society of loving neighbors. Religion remains the dominant institution pressuring for such change and for presenting a hopeful attitude.

God's creation, our self-organizing, self-maintaining, self-healing world, is moving in time toward what we hope is a convergence toward a God- purpose. The evolutionary history of earth and Man is the story of God's creation, a story lasting 14 billion years, with the story of life being about the last 4 billion years of the 14. The first stories of the *Bible* are thought to have been written down about 900 Bc. We have added 2000 more years to that written history of our religion. It is as important to study and find God's purpose in this history of our creation as it is the words of the *Bible*. God's universe is full of awe and meaning, and needs to be elevated with *the Bible*, not left to become irrelevant. Our progress in finding God's intent in his creation will be, in large part, in the limiting or elimination of self-defeating behavior which interferes with the foundational Christian message of love.

We think about the God-man and the Man-God in Jesus. The particle/wave metaphor of quantum physics expresses this paradox. Once recognized it took at least two generations to accept the particle/wave phenomenon as physics. We must not be too demanding of science in dealing with Jesus. There is another phenomenon of science that we think of as fractals. Fractals are self- similar patterns whether observed from near or far. They occur in many structures in our world. A fern leaf is often mentioned. One that I have begun to think about extends from the macrocosm to the microcosm. Scientists are telling us that the expanding universe is the result of the gravitational dynamic of dark matter and dark energy that is composed of 95% of the mass of our universe. That is, only 5% is the stuff of stars and planets, and of ourselves is physical substance as we know it.

It has been said that 95% of the Mind is the unconscious Mind and that 5% is the conscious Mind. If the 95% of dark matter is controlling the expansion of the universe, is it not plausible that the 95% of the God of the unconscious Mind is controlling the evolution of life? The neutrinos that have negligible mass, in their quadrillions are thought to make up the mass of dark matter. Is it implausible that the quadrillions of living organisms make up the dynamic of evolution, guided by the God of Mind: awareness of environment to self- awareness to awareness of others?

Only the mind can match the cosmos in its numbers of synapses, the stars of the brain. Study of science has brought us through technology to the brink of godhood. It seems that technology has outrun our human capacity for self- regulation. We have the capacity to choose either evolution or extinction. The behavior of a few will make that decision. It is the nature of our gift of freedom and choice. The choice for god-regulation has become an almost physical necessity. Love of neighbor becomes the new survival behavior.

CHAPTER VIII

BIBLE VS. CREATION

If we believe that God is the creator of our universe, and we believe that the *Bible* is the word of God, then the two must be congruent. The *Bible* carries the message of God's intent, a God purpose. That purpose, according to the *Bible*, presents humanity as central to God's purpose. To fulfill God's purpose requires man's survival as a primary requisite. We would expect that God's universe, however created, has the potential to fulfill God's purpose. Humanity, its changing environment and its evolutionary history to this point has been required to fulfill God's purpose. We would expect that God's plan (purpose) would converge on God's creation at a conjunction where God's intent is fulfilled. We humans are agents in God's fulfillment plan, or could it be more than that? Perhaps we will evolve to gain the skills and abilities to perform acts that fulfill God's intent. Perhaps we will evolve to become the object of his fulfillment.

We are not God's word. We are God's creation in the created universe. The Bible tells us that our function is to build loving relationships and that this is above the law and the insights of our prophets. The mission of life for four billion years has been to survive. We have survived to a complexity to imagine God. The mechanism for this imagining is the human brain that sits at the top of the evolutionary complexity pyramid. It is through mind that we make a spiritual connection with God. It is through belief in God that we find the hope that sustains motivation toward a meaningful purpose, giving value to our being. We are part of something larger than ourselves. We are self- transcendent if we choose that. Self-transcendence is a universal idea. Our path is through the teachings of Jesus.

I have said many times that evolution is God's creation tool. The resulting diversity has created a world that is sometimes directed towards God's purpose and sometimes directed in opposition to God's purpose. To date, it seems that there has been a net positive convergence toward a humanity that is both aware and self aware, a humanity with the ability to imagine God, if we choose to do so. The problem with diversity as a universal result of evolution is that it is natural for the existence of both good and bad, whatever our measure. Bad in the broad sense is opposition to God's intent. This would be for us, opposition to the building of loving relationships. This opposition is primarily driven by man's potential for survival behavior: ego defense mechanisms such as tantrums and blaming, control psychology, and illogical, self-defeating behavior. These systems and processes are a part of God's creation package, accepted as the price for net positive progress toward a God purpose.

As we move toward greater and greater knowledge of how the world works, we begin to sense a convergence of science and religion, particularly in the realm of brain and mind. The physical working, the chemistry and physics, of the brain in unknown ways creates consciousness and mind. These are not measurable and can not be said to be scientific, but they are supported by physical and chemical processes. Yet there is an ability to create ideas through exposure to other ideas, both within an individual and between groups. It is as though ideas can infect other ideas within the brain as pure thought and between brains through some physical communication means. This ability to comprehend ideas, to assimilate and to create new ideas is a non-real spiritual component of our being. As we face the continued evolution of our specie, we expect that while brain change will be immeasurably slow, we will experience incredibly rapid evolution of information and mind.

It seems that in addition to our historic elevation of the *Bible* as the authority on Christianity, the result of the information explosion and its impact on mind will support the elevation of the created world and the way the world works, to become an equally important authority in support of God's intent. It is through brain, and mind, that we come to know God and it is through brain, and mind, that we will come to know his creation. We know God through Jesus and/or Jesus' work. Can we know God through God's other work, his creation? Wisdom comes through experiencing God's creation.

CHAPTER IX

SEARCHING FOR BALANCE

About seventy percent of adult Americans say that they believe in God, but only about sixty percent of these attend church on a typical Sunday. Only 20 percent of adult Americans believe that community is an essential part of their spiritual growth. We want to be 'spiritual' and we want to be accepted by God, but we're not sure we want him controlling our lives and adjusting the identity that we've become so attached to.

We remain unconvinced of the necessity of a spiritual environment. This is partially because church finances force us to focus on attendance rather than relationships and immersion. It is also due to our instinct to protect our freedom and choice. We cannot forget the less than welcome experiences that are part of any group process, but that, in churches, conflict with our expectations.

There would appear to be a sense of danger in getting sucked into a cult- like environment with obligations beyond our willingness to accept and beyond our capacity to refuse. Real or perceived, the resulting anxiety is stifling and eliminates commitment. Is it possible to provide community spiritual growth in balance with the needs of members? Is it possible to sustain a community of faith without the threat of excessive obligation? Is it possible to provide real or perceived benefits to members that make members' commitment justified in their own view? How do we help members to realize their positive expectations?

Moderation has been a historical theme in religion since the time of the Restoration. Thinking of a normal distribution in behavior, moderation would suggest establishing ourselves around the central tendency, in the middle but toward the positive side. That is, more good than, rather than mostly good or mostly bad. This seems a reasonable compromise for balance. Our current society is anything but moderate. There is the beginning of a swell toward escape from our frenetic information overload into modes of silence such as meditation that suggest opportunities for religious communities.

Our Government and financial systems are expected to have a suitable ethic, likely universalism that compliments their behavior as living systems. In fact, we find that our problems are the result of a lack of any ethics, no moral restraint. The answer to why those we put in control put us in danger, aside from greed, is "Because I can". Why do they not fix problems that are obvious to everyone? Because the sub-systems that are supposed to act as a check and balance, sacrifice the Nation's objectives to fulfill their own objectives. These people are not mentally challenged. Their balancing act is, "How much can I get before the system collapses?" That is why all living systems require some balance between freedom and control.

The system breaks when those in charge also get to control regulation. This game is played in all living systems. No living system is immune, not government, not corporations, not religion. Illogical self-defeating behavior is a common natural phenomenon. Religion is a dominant force in pressuring for an ethic of intrinsic rightness. How could we possibly feel that religion is not needed? Is it not obvious? Balance involves the ethic of universalism as the primary ethic coupled with an ethic of intrinsic rightness to adjust for any disparity. The result is stability. We can talk about the ethical judgment as a philosophy, outside of religion, but without a religious environment, we complex human systems, by nature, adapt to our environment whatever that may be. Our Congress is a good example.

Chapter X

Separation

Sitting in a meeting recently, I asked how many believed in God. Everyone raised their hand in affirmation. When I asked how many went to church, considerably less than half said yes. It seems clear that many have a disconnection between God and church. How does one believe in God and not believe in its primary institutions in our culture? If they believe in church, why don't they attend? If they attend why don't they feel more responsible for supporting the mission of church? I have had many church goers admit that they don't believe much of the dogma, liturgy and/or tradition of the church. Occasionally, churched people admit that they have trouble believing in God. Given the diversity of nature we would expect members to attend or not attend church for a variety of personal reasons unrelated to church teaching and practice.

If we are committed to our church, then we need to seek understanding in the nature of the relationships members have with their church. We also need to understand the nature of non-member believers' relationship with church. Surveys indicate a significant drop in church membership, and also a move of young adults toward spiritualism, that is often spiritual practice without a god. Many, probably most, of us have had events in our lives that led us in and out of periods of greater and less focus on religious life.

There are countless examples of events that separate us from God. The recent biography of Steve Jobs by Walter Isaacson mentions Steve's early challenge. At the age of thirteen, he rejected God for not preventing starvation in Biafra. This is the dilemma of unrealistic expectations. In doing so, Steve never went back to church. He later pursued Zen Buddhism. "He said that religion was at its best when it emphasized spiritual experience rather than received dogma." "The juice goes out of Christianity when it becomes too based on faith rather than on living like Jesus or seeing the world as Jesus saw it." This is perhaps another way of saying that actions speak louder than words. We need to see our real world and look at the ways in which it supports Jesus' works. If we can't do that, there is no passion, no emotional experience and no motivation to change. Our alternative is apt to be to avoid the church to relieve our cognitive dissonance.

The church as a religious institution is expected to operate in a state of divine grace. As a typical complex living system, it suffers the impact of humanity as do other organizations. The nature of bureaucratic practice is human, not divine. It is people-run, not God-run, in spite of its attempt to be guided by divine will. In placing God in control of all of Nature, we find ourselves searching for justification for God's allowance of pestilence, war and general mayhem. We can say that he has a divine plan for the death of innocence, but that buys little room in today's modern world. We blame God. In so doing we separate ourselves from God. In separating ourselves from religious practice, we separate ourselves from religious thought. This reduction in religious thought, acts on our brain's learning process: "Use it or lose it." Religion at its best is an immersion process. Belief takes the work of constant repetition. True belief is both talking the talk and walking the walk.

Perhaps one way to become aware of the importance of church is to speculate on the impact if the church were eliminated. Is there a better institution to provide its goods and services: corporations… foundations… government? One answer to atheism and supporting organizations might be to close down all religious activity for a period of a month or so. Imagine the chaos.

CHAPTER XI

THE CREATION GAP

Life is full of gaps. There is a gap between what we should do and what we do. There is a gap between what we expect and what we get. There is a gap between what we want and what we need. There is a gap between the events in our lives and our ability to deal with them. There is a gap between what we get in life and what we give. Life is full of gaps. Some gaps relate to individuals, some to groups. Some gaps evolve with culture, with changing environments. This book is about the creation gap. After writing the book, *Who Me?*, I began to ask my self why I wrote it. I thought that I was writing it to give others a different view of life. Actually, I have come to believe that I wrote it to help me understand my own view and my own gaps.

I am haunted by the gap between what I observe about people practicing their religion and my expectation about what that practice should look like based on the liturgy. It occurs to me that we are the created, doing what the created do when placed in a diversity of environments with a diversity of skills and abilities. We do what God expects us to do, in our particular situation. After all he created us. Our expectations are learned through traditional religious training. We are given the Bible as "The Word of God". That this idea reverberates through the centuries is undeniable. We are given stories about God's interaction with Man, Man's interaction with God, and Man's interaction with Man. We are given that the "World" is evil and that we are rotten to the core with sin. It is Man's duty to reject worldly things and, through the good news of the *Gospel,* find salvation in Jesus Christ. This seems to have the ring of truth in the face of the general and continuous mayhem that has gone on throughout history.

At some point we begin to wonder what life is all about. We begin asking existentialist questions. If God created the world, why is it evil? If God is God, why has it taken nearly 4 billion years for life to evolve to us? Why evolution? Why not 'Zap'? The process of evolution goes on beyond us. Why do we think that we are the apex of a convergence? If the span of all life were treated as a single day, 24 hours, humanity would come on the scene in the last minute or so. Is there a convergence? We are still behaving more animal like than human. Does God have a plan? Our ideas about God and Jesus were developed in a primitive culture and became relatively diverse during the first 300 years before it was legalized, and then held constant for about 1200 years by isolating erudition to a very few. We are diverse again, free to think what we think, do what we do. Unfortunately, what we do is often counter to any conceivable God purpose.

By the 16th-17th century, Church control began to crack. Biblical logic became unsustainable in the face of observation of God's creation. The Church presented itself as the authority on all knowledge. The idea that the sun revolved around the earth was typical dogma. In our time and since the early 20th century, advances in the study of God's creation, science, is forcing us to again rethink our religious traditions. We have discovered much of how the world works, and particularly how the human mind works. Archeological finds conflict with historical references. Rigorous analysis of the Bible using document validation tools is providing insights that weaken belief in its inerrancy. Computer technology has made knowledge of all these advances universally available.

We are now discovering that the works of God, his creation, the what, are as important as the words of God in the Bible, the how to. With the development of molecular biology and MRI scanning of the brain over the last 40 years, scientific study of the brain and mind has brought new life to what some call the last frontier in medicine. Nearly 20 centuries of focus on Biblical theology has made religious discussion of the created world nearly irrelevant. Third century dogma could not survive the 16th century. 16th century dogma is unlikely to survive the 21st century. How do we close the gap between literal biblical teaching and the facts of creation, the way God's world works? What is the path for integration of God's words and God's works?

How will this flood of new insights into the brain and mind impact religion? It is the Author's expectation that there will be integration, a closing of the gap, eliminating much of the cognitive dissonance that leads to religious instability. This integration must come from a new awareness of the language of creation and recognition that it is one with the message of the *Bible*. The result will likely be a unifying message of loving relationships that stabilizes a diverse majority of the population. Given the nature of complex living systems, we need to celebrate diversity, not repress it. Again, it is God created. The Author expects that this integration will give added power to the biblical message, freeing it from dated ideas and dated culture. How can God's word not be reflected in God's works?

Chapter XII

The Church

Many think that the church is not essential for belief in God. This can be true, but those who can maintain a strong belief without the support of like- minded people are relatively rare. The idea of religion outside of a religious environment suggests an inability to self-transcend, a fundamental precept of all religions. In a practical sense, they overlook the fact that great ideas are spread through the leverage of large groups of like-minded people.

Why are traditional churches losing membership? Have we lost the will to immerse ourselves in the ideas and processes of learning to believe? Spiritual growth is work. Many think that attending church on Sunday is sufficient. While we appear to have an instinctive need for a spiritual component in our life, without some self-transcendent motivational event, we forgo the work of spiritual growth for more pleasurable activity. Pleasure is an individual and momentary emotion. "Success breeds forgetting." "Familiarity breeds contempt". These insights take on meaning with the wisdom of experience. We need to think more about what transcendent motivational events might be.

Stewardship is part of church life. It can be a stressful part, dependent on our expectations. Church membership has trended downward long enough to suggest that the church has systemic problems. What people will support financially is certainly an indication of its relevance in their lives. Churches struggle to find a balance between large numbers of members giving low dollar amounts and few members giving high dollar amounts. Power law (80- 20 rule) applies and is representative of the diversity in pledge amounts. Tithing is the obvious solution, but a 3x increase in average giving requires a generational learning process.

Small traditional churches with big properties are paying 95% of expenses to operate the church and 5% on missions. Churches do not think of the support of their own congregation as a mission. Missions should transcend self. Yet, almost all of their income is consumed in support of ministering to their own congregations. Net income only covers a fraction of expenses. Most of these churches have scraped the bottom of the barrel in searching for cost reduction and special project incomes. This leaves them with two key tasks: 1) increasing the average pledge income, and 2) increasing the membership.

When we talk about increasing church income we find it hard to find enthusiastic faces. In the Bible, 'the well' is a common scene for obtaining a drink or finding a wife. Going back to the well today brings forth no such happy thoughts. This familiarity does indeed seem to breed contempt. Members become immune, resentful of stewardship talk. Transparency is not particularly effective. Number presentations in their simplest form make little impact on the average member. If pricing is in large part set by customer need, it seems that we are not presenting the right product, or we are presenting the right product in the wrong way. Traditional small churches exist in the presence of small growing churches that start out in a neighborhood house and grow magically. What seems true is that these churches start with a balanced budget and an excess of desired services. Their budget grows in balance with their growing membership. This is complemented by the attribute of newness that is motivational. Their association with success breeds a passion for the confirmation of continued growth.

If the spiritual need is real, then we are forced to find new ways of presenting our selves as a church. Jesus said that the first and second commandment supersede the law and the prophets. The primary presentation might then be the promise of loving relationships. The second might be the resurrection story. The first deals with this life, the second with a next life. We might think of the value of "now" vs. "later". Both God and resurrection are spiritual, mental constructs that are beyond understanding, but maintained by belief through faith. Love is also a mental construct, but is experienced in this life. In all three concepts, the idea is learned and then expressed as behavior in this life.

Both God and resurrection are counter-intuitive, other worldly, spiritual ideas. They fight for understanding in our current culture of science and technology. Loving relationship suffers the confusion between the effortless pleasurable emotion of being in love, and that love that is the work and sometimes pain of growing spiritually with others. With the divorce rate around 50%, and marriage as a sacrament, the church finds itself caught in a crack, appearing ineffective. The church is not in the psychotherapy business. The Church finds itself as a partner in a dance with science and technology, and without dance lessons.

Perhaps we need a different way to approach the adaptation challenge of Modern Christianity. We consider the Bible as God's word and the only reference required to live a Christian life. In this consideration we also acknowledge God as The Creator. As a primitive document, the *Bible* content fits its environment of origin. Two millennia later, we are struggling to preserve the message of the *Bible* while adjusting the meaning with historical insights. This is complicated by whole world visibility in a world with cultures ranging from pre-Christian to post modern. The *Bible* ranges from literal to metaphorical. We are struggling to make *Bible* teaching fit with 21st century culture. If we perceive the *Bible* as the word of God, why can't we perceive the universe and our being in it as works of God?

Logically, the works of God should support the words of God. Equally important, the words of God should support the works of God. The historical elevation of the *Bible* represents a sacred paradigm. Change is pain. Yet, all the living and non-living systems and processes of our universe are the works of God. Science is the study of God's creation, made available to us through his process of evolution, culminating in the human brain and mind. The new observations about God's world are minimized by our instinct to protect what we currently know, as though it were who we are. Ultimately truth prevails.

Why do we continually find ourselves struggling to make the world fit biblical logic? A well known strategy is, "If you can't fight them, join them". Scientists' discoveries define God's works. Claim them as God's works. Forget proofs of His existence. Forget intelligent design. There isn't any logical or any evidential proof of God. If you want to lead, get in front of the parade. Given this as an optional path, should we not test its possibilities?

When we begin to look at the larger picture of God's creation, the way the world works, we get a different or expanded picture of our growth problems. In the last two centuries, the average number of children per family has reduced twice, from 7 to 3.5 to 1.75. Small children (our cradle Christians) are in their fastest learning years and easily imprinted for life. At this point, we don't have enough children per family to maintain the culture, let alone Christianity. Young adults seem a growth possibility, but that becomes as much an un-imprinting as an imprinting task that is energy draining. Also, our traditional churches are not designed for today's youth.

If we add to this that the senior population is the fastest growing segment, we can reduce our potential child membership per family by another 50%. We begin to realize that "what used to be" was a Christianity fed by the fossil fuel of imprinted children. We have lost our fuel supply. Just these two factors are sufficient to get us to today's average parish church picture. If we further add that our churches were built for 300 members, the 50-100 members today need to triple in membership to support the cost of operation. This is unlikely to happen. It is a gut-wrenching fact. Adapt or die.

For us, the customer base of cradle Christians has disappeared with the buggy whip. Perhaps our present focus should be on the physical plant. Our churches were not built to adapt to our present market. With new architecture, audiovisual systems and computer programming, liturgy will adapt. To renew our fossil fuel, we need to fund the transition to our new environment. We can't afford to fund the past. We don't live there anymore.

The biblical message to separate yourself from the world in order to claim your presence with God, colors God's creation black. It might be equally read as giving up your self-defeating behaviors and claiming the self-enhancing behaviors that God intended. This is also a resurrection process. We are offered the freedom and choice to do this, but it is not an equal opportunity process. It requires work to love God, self and others. We are given the gift of freedom to choose the better way. Our choices represent the history of our lives and are a measure of life's meaning. What is such a gift worth? How do we value a life worth living? Where do we find such an environment? If it is not available, should we not participate in the making of such an environment? Such environments are called churches.

Chapter XIII

Our Competitive Edge

Religion is a system of ideas that has evolved recently in the evolution of mind. A fundamental result of religion is giving human life meaning. Christians believe that this is accomplished by creating loving relationships. That is, loving relationship with God, with neighbor, with self, and presumably with our environment. Worship is made up of the diversity of ideas and tools for religious practice.

What then is the most efficient way to create loving relationships? This process today is wrapped in so much liturgy and dogma that most of our energy and assets go into maintaining the vehicle that carries the process. Is evangelism only for fundamentalist churches? Can we facilitate the spiritual growth of existing membership? Can we facilitate evangelism… Both? One can believe that fundamentalists have a passion for their work. Can we imagine parishes having a passion for spiritually growing existing members? How do we create this passion? It seems that passion is generated for what is exciting and new. Do we need new ways to present our message? Passion is infectious. Can we find a core of passionate people willing to infect their fellow members? Good infects bad. Bad infects good. That is the nature and impact of stored learning on human behavior. We know that illogical, self- defeating behavior limits or eliminates loving relationships

The evolution of mind might be divided into pre-human, human and post- human. The pre-human mind is primarily animal in nature, survival driven and aware only of its own environment. The human mind is aware of both environment and self. Its primary struggle is in building and retaining its own identity. Post-human mind is transcendent. It is expressed in a society characterized by loving relationships. We might then characterize our own group evolutionary status of mind as human with a large helping of pre-human and a small helping of post-human behavior. Our challenge is to survive long enough to become predominantly post-human. This is God's creation message: survive; all are one; love one another.

There is still the real possibility of a small group of pre-human mind types with behaviors that will destroy us and themselves in their quest for survival of their own ideas. It is our nature to build hierarchal structures. Controlling personalities are drawn to such structures to express their pre-human behavior. Power corrupts. All corporate forms, including churches, are subject to such personalities. Our society is both complex and diverse. As Christians, we have the responsibility for a passionate commitment to regain our competitive edge as a vibrant cultural institution. It is such institutions that provide pressure for a stable balance between self-transcendent and survival behavior.

CHAPTER XIV

CHURCH IDENTITY CRISIS

The membership of traditional churches has been falling for decades. The usual answer is that there is too much competition for our limited time: TV, Sports, Jobs, etc. If we are losing members, or not gaining members, we have to assume that what we offer is not competitive. Churches tend to update their literature to make it current, but this has not proven very effective. Trends show that people attend church for recreation, rather than **re**-creation. Attempts to add the benefits of recreation would seem to move us further in the direction of culture defined churches, rather than toward church defined cultures.

Changing to follow cultural change is a natural system directive of adaptation, but it can endanger our sense of who we are, our identity as a church. If we have nothing to offer, we should fade away. If we have a worthy offering, we should make a passionate commitment to support that offering. If we have changed or the culture has changed in ways that obscure our identity, then we must make it again clear who we are. Our identity, or at least its message, should be neither time dependent, nor culture dependent. Can we have an identity that is eternal, free of environmental change?

Who were we that religion was so fundamental to our culture in the past? Church growth has been dependent as much on violent action as compassion. Central to our cultural evolution has been the control psychology that both manipulates and advances religion. Perhaps the requirements for growth are in conflict with our message of love and compassion. Can we be zealots in teaching compassion? That seems to be what made St. Paul and Mother Theresa successful. Zealous leadership involves passionate belief. How do we create a loving passion? Passion coupled with belief is both inward and outward directed. It both minimizes self-need and takes responsibility for the needs of others. St. Paul was taking a new idea to a needy population. Mother Theresa was taking physical safety to a needy population. We are taking a 2000 year old message to an indifferent population. It seems that it is the unique, pious few individuals who in each generation remind us what it means to be religious. What processes evolve these individuals with the ability to inspire us to give meaning to our lives? Why do some people have the spark of holiness while others do not? Where does empathy and compassion come from? What part of these attributes is genetic and what part experiential? Can we learn commitment to religion or is it instinctive? How much of such learning is required to ensure the survival of our Church, of Christianity? How do we teach a passion for religion?

It seems that each parish, more or less, follows the 80-20 rule. How are the 20 percent that carry 80 percent of the weight different from the 80 percent? How do we attract these people? Are some people more susceptible than others? Is this susceptibility learned or is it instinctive? Perhaps there is a threshold of religious activity that imprints some with religion as a quality image in their mind. It seems clear that we are what we do and do what we are. Thus, we ultimately know them by their actions. Perhaps one strategy is to define a minimum behavioral goal and move members to that threshold. Without a minimum goal, we have no strategy and likely no movement toward that goal.

At some level, time and effort become immersion. We need to be careful of words like immersion. It has the flavor of 'born again'. How do you tell people that to have a successful church you need to spend more than one or two hours a week? A tithing policy is becoming an important issue as we struggle with small deficit-ridden parishes. The more time and money invested in something, the more you value it. It would seem its corollary is that the less time and money you invest, the less you value it.

Is who we are obsolete, or has who we are been obscured by change in our culture? As we become more and more needy, we lose our mission of support for others, and direct our energy at sustaining ourselves. As our energies are consumed in supporting self, we loose our identity and mission as a church. We no longer attend to others. Attending to others gives meaning to life. Without meaning our identity, our purpose, becomes obscure. Driven by deficit budgets, we tend to think about moving into areas where we are less competitive. This is a cyclical process that will consume us.

It would seem to be a mistake to move religious activity toward recreation. We are then choosing to compete with other recreational entities that have different rules. This constitutes a change in identity. Recreation can be used to draw new members, but its basis is self-gratification. Our identity as a church must be self-transcendent. In building relationships, we transcend self. Meaning is about building relationships.

Relationship building must be a critical part of our sense of self. Maintaining a balance is also critical. We are a part of our greater system culture. As such, we must be concerned with how much of our energies can be directed at the greater system without negatively impacting our own identity and mission as parishes. As the greater system of our own sub- systems, our members, we also must be concerned with the energy balance that stabilizes those relationships.

We hear a lot about atheism these days. We are challenged to eliminate religious symbols from public buildings and grounds. This activity appears as an issue of separation of church and state. Actually, these ideas are about the fear that religious belief, or any belief system can be used as a way of taking away our freedom. We have the history to validate this concern. In the short term, atheism is more likely to take away our freedom than religion taking away government's control.

Freedom and choice are instinctive. They are precious to us and challenging them elicits survival behavior. It seems that any means to recreate a quality image of religion in the mind would ensure a high place for freedom and choice. We are encouraged to live in the present, having the freedom to say what we say, think what we think, see what we see, hear what we hear and feel what we feel. We need the freedom to think about and discuss all aspects of religious life. To do less leaves us with a host of discordant thoughts, struggling with the gap between what we experience and what we are taught. It is impractical in our age of information to accept belief as a dictum.

God is love. Love is a behavior. Behavior is in large part shaped by stored learning from past events. Love is the commitment to the spiritual growth of self and others. Commitment to spiritual growth is primarily expressed by listening to and attending to. Christian love is about relationship building. What is it that limits or eliminates relationship building? We let ourselves become too self-oriented, a natural consequence of our survival imperative. This leaves us open to all sorts of opportunities for instant gratification. The silent impact of a move toward less religious activity becomes the loss of religion as a quality image. Disuse causes erosion of mental attributes, much the same way as with muscle.

As we build relationships in search of meaning in our lives, we are faced with a diversity of events that we are called to deal with. We understand that, given our varied skills and abilities, we are called within the confines of our particular identity. Nonetheless, we are constantly called to make choices. The history of our lives is the sum of the choices we have made. Still, successful choices can result in elevating ones self-esteem without giving life meaning. Wealth is desirable. It offers confirmation, but does not guarantee happiness. Meaning in life involves self-transcendence and that involves relationships. We are social creatures. Success without sharing is hollow. It is not a large leap to realize that shared successes can grow church membership. It is hard to say enough about the power of positive thinking. We are each a mixed bag of self-enhancing and self-defeating attitudes that slip in and out of our behavior. We know that repetition is a learning process. Repetition of life-enhancing experience leads to life-enhancing behavior. Early on we learned, "If you can't say something nice, don't say anything at all"; "Laugh and the world laughs with you. Cry and you cry alone." Smiles elicit smiles;

anger elicits anger. A safe and welcoming environment is critical for growth. The choice of people to represent the face of a church should be obvious. Availability of such welcoming talent is the problem. We are left to try to train members that in some seems to be an inborn gift. Positive thinking leads to self-enhancing behavior.

CHAPTER XV
COGNITIVE DISSONANCE

Who am I? Who am I not? When a threatening event causes me stress, I get angry. What in the event elicits that anger? There is a gap between my expectations and perceptions, and what I am experiencing. Apparently, my expectations and perceptions are, at least, a significant part of who I am. If an event elicits no such emotion, then that event is unlikely to be a significant part of who I am. Or perhaps, it is a significant part of who I am not. We tend to get what we expect. It seems then that our expectations and perceptions that feed our emotions result in behaviors that define us. Our behavior is a projection of our stored learning. Challenge to that learning is a challenge to who we are. We respond with survival behavior, protecting those expectations and perceptions.

New learning is not a challenge unless it implies change to our old learning. That is, our sense of whom we are. New learning requires work. If we are stressed by feelings of being over-worked, new learning can be perceived as a challenge and elicit a survival response. Daily events that are transient can create a survival response. Clearly our ability to control our survival response to challenging events also defines us. What we can control, we can avoid projecting as our behavior. We can be generally good natured, or generally bad natured, generally productive, or generally unproductive. The glass may be half full, or half empty. Are we motivated to change? Our ability to learn is at its peak in the first 10 years of life. Since our identity is relatively complete by the age of 5-6, it seems that a majority of our primary formative experiences are related to skills in parenting. Tantrums effective in childhood are not uncommon in adult behavior.

"Laugh and the world laughs with you. Cry and you cry alone." Who we are impacts our relationships. Our expectations and perceptions are generally realized. Aware or not, we recreate around us the environment and culture in which we live, through our behavior. Events that are the most impacting on us are those that challenge our sense of self. Hurt and embarrassment imprint deeply, lowering our self-esteem. Low self-esteem interferes with our ability to sift out misfit, childhood learning with the filter of adult logic.

We approach adulthood with a mixed bag of positive and negative behaviors. We tend to be known by one or two dominant behaviors. We function in our profession in relationship to the fit of these behaviors. Through immersion in the subject of our profession, we gain an acceptable level of skill and knowledge for progressing. We are not generally aware that this immersion process is an essential part of ownership in any knowledge or skill area. Immersion is a process of learning that results in knowing, ownership and belief. Repetition is a key part of this process. It is the way memory creation works in our mental learning system.

What happens when we find that what we learned as truth becomes clearly untrue? We can accept some level of this cognitive dissonance. We can accept this as a signal for change and make the effort to change. We can create an excuse to justify inaction. In dealing with these options, we consider the advantages of maintaining the status quo vs. change. What is the value of an historical but false position vs. the value of a current and truthful position? If change is required, change what… change how… and at what rate? Rates of change are critical. What will be the collateral damage? There are always unintended consequences. What is the risk in changing?

The mind experiences cognitive dissonance when it becomes aware of ideas that are catalogued as truth when they are obviously untrue. Yet, there are mental processes that seem to be evolved to avoid cognitive dissonance. How can a person educated in a particular area believe what his senses convey as false? The brain rejects what does not fit its previous learning. The brain seeks the pleasure of confirmation of its current stored learning. In justification, "everyone is doing it". Information contrary to belief is met with the coping behaviors of denial, negation, blaming and transference which are among the group of ego defense mechanisms that reduce cognitive dissonance. The brain has evolved to treat facts and ideas in different parts of the brain. What you believe is true becomes true for you. This attribute of mind has been responsible in large part for the success of religion. It is only in the past 50 years or so in the modern world that we have begun to pay a price for that success.

We find ourselves in an epic flood of new information that is altering our environment at a rate that challenges our capacity to adapt, as individuals and as a culture. Our technology is growing at a pace that is mind numbing as well as physically threatening. Our dominant emotions are confusion, frustration, hopelessness and fear. Our individual freedoms are at risk. Poverty is rampant and our religions under attack. Corporate greed and corruption are at epic proportions. Our National identity is fracturing. Our ability to adapt as individuals, as groups and as a Nation is floundering. What is going on? What are the causative events? What do we have to do to gain control: revert to the past; live in the present; hope for future change?

This need for change is echoing through all aspects of our culture. The language speaks clearly: Education: "The dumbing of America"; Finance: "The Occupation of Wall Street"; Congress: "The Banks own the Congress"; Culture: "Holiday Tree?" Religion: "No public expression allowed", Illegal immigration: "Equal Rights." It can not be coincidence that this infection is impacting all aspects of our Society. The problem is systemic. It is felt in traditional churches as a long term trend of lost membership, a trend toward spiritualism, secular humanism, and toward recreation as a form of worship. The stress, the tension, the cognitive dissonance we experience is an alarm bell, signaling the need for change. This cultural systemic infection involves a general loss of identity. Identity is the reference we use in determining the relevance of new information. Our learning system cannot adapt to the epic flood of information we are experiencing. It represents a breakdown in the information pathways, the webs of relationships that stabilize our being as complex living systems.

As we think about religious issues in the context of System's Theory, it is easy to slip into the same discussion about our Government, or Wall Street, or corporations. I write about them interchangeably. The reason is that all living systems follow the same systems rules. They evolve, grow, age and die through similar processes using the same rules. They all fit the same self- organizing, layered structural model, using the same webs of information pathways (relationships). They all follow the same path to death when those information pathways become clogged, making it impossible to respond to critical information. They all depend on a strong identity to interpret information. Loss of identity leads to poor and sluggish responses that herald extinction.

CHAPTER XVI

COMPLEXITY

A concern of mine is that people often utilize science as justification for disbelief in God. Our universe is an unknowably complex system that operates according to system rules. Discovery of various rule sets neither elevates man, nor diminishes God.

A consequence of large parallel computer systems was the observation that identical small programs (distributive agents) working together tend to offer unintended and unexpected results. Study of a variety of these now recognized "distributive agent systems" has led to the development of complexity theory. The basic premise of complexity theory is that there is a hidden order to the behavior of complex systems, whether that system is an ecosystem, a national economy, an organization, or a human being. If left to function on their own, these systems tend to organize themselves.

Proponents of complexity theory believe specific traits are shared by most complex systems. These systems are the combination of many independent agents behaving as a single unit. These agents respond to their environment, much as genes respond to natural selection. Networks of agents act as a single system made up of many interacting component sub-systems. Complexity Theory attempts to explain how even millions of independent agents can unintentionally demonstrate patterned behavior and properties that, while present in the overall system, are not present in any individual component of that system.

Of self-organizing behaviors, two are of particular interest in the study of evolution. One is adaptation. It is believed that the ability to adapt is characteristic of complex systems and maybe one reason why evolution seems to lead toward complex organisms. Of more importance is the way complex systems seem to strike a balance between the need for order and the imperative to change. Complex systems tend to locate themselves at a place called "the edge of chaos". Imagine "the edge of chaos" as a place where there is enough innovation to keep a living system vibrant, and enough stability to keep it from collapsing into anarchy. It is a zone of conflict and upheaval where the old and the new are constantly at war.

Finding the balance point must be a delicate matter. If a living system drifts too close to the edge, it risks falling over into incoherence and dissolution; but if the system moves too far away from the edge, it becomes rigid, frozen, and totalitarian. Both conditions lead to extinction. Too much change is as destructive as too little. The implication is that extinction is the inevitable result of one or the other strategy—too much change or too little.

The complex systems best able to adapt to their environment are most likely to survive. Over time it is predictable that complex systems would learn to both adapt to changing environments, and change their environment to suit their system needs. This dual process presents the potential for the environment to change at a faster rate than the ability of complex systems to adapt. Since environmental change is controlled (at least initially) by the complex system, extinction is also, to that extent, controlled by the complex system. This suggests that in later stages of complexity, extinction is dependent on the balance between rates of change, rather than change itself.

Continuous evolution of a system may exhaust its support system. It would either become extinct or revert to an earlier state of evolution. The time to adapt would be critical. As complex systems continue to evolve, the issue arises whether complexity itself may become so evolved as to become self-defeating. This would suggest that various processes were unable to evolve at the same rate as the primary system. The more complex a system is, the greater the number of processes and the more difficult its orchestration.

Self-organization in complex systems occurs as a natural process. Schooling of fish, insect swarms and flocking of birds are examples. Studies show that such phenomena have no leaders and no system level controls. At the agent level, instincts like "stay close together" and "fly in the same general direction as the group", are sufficient to establish the flocking. Artificial intelligence programming (top down directives) to accomplish flocking would require programs as large as to be impractical. Distributive agent systems are the result of organisms/agents constantly adapting to each other. They adapt in ways that benefit themselves and in so doing optimize the system.

Diversity is a natural result of evolution. Adaptation in these continuous evolving systems results in diversity at all levels. As an example, a foreign antigen in the body will result in the production of antibodies with a range of sensitivity and specificity. This diversity has an umbrella effect that covers a range of potential adaptations of the antigen.

Perhaps the most consistent adaptation that presents a threat to the system is complexity itself. Conservation of energy is a law of nature. Greater complexity requires greater energy. More efficient systems are an obvious answer, but system efficiency tends to be at the expense of freedom and choice. This, in turn, interferes with the free interaction of the agents that defines the system. The overly complex system is forced to revert to an earlier more stable form, or face extinction. The stress associated with positioning at "the edge of chaos" may motivate creative solutions, but requires greater energy. Balancing at the edge of chaos is thought by some to be the system's most effective positioning.

Because the system is dependent on so many intricate interactions, the number of possible reactions to any given change is infinite. Minor events can have enormous consequences because of the chain of reactions they might incite (butterfly effect). Conversely, major changes may have an almost insignificant effect on the system as a whole. Because of these unpredictable consequences, strong control of any complex system may be impossible. While the complex system may have order, no one can govern with certainty a complex system.

Complexity Theory is one aspect of General Systems Theory. As a logical presentation of a concept, it can be called a theory and will remain so until proven false. Complexity Theory is an aspect of evolution, as diversity is, in turn, an aspect of evolution. Diversity increases the variety of distributive agents. With increasing numbers of distributive agents, a system may take on characteristics that are not typical of the distributive agents as individuals or as sub-groups.

It all seems to have started with the Big Bang. We are apt to think of the Big Bang as an explosion somewhere in time and space. Before the Big Bang there was no time and no space. There was also no oxygen. This was not an explosion of the type we tend to think of. The Big Bang brought with it time and space in what that theory suggests was an instantaneous expansion.

From this dawning in time, one might visualize the beginning as a sea of energy. Within this activity, possibly in the first few second, some of the energy began to take on the character of particles. These particle-like patterns of energy evolved properties of spin and angularity, along with positive and negative charge. This activity evolved into hydrogen and helium atoms. Gravity captured this matter into giant stars. As the fusion energy of giant stars was used up these stars collapsed under gravitational force to become neutron stars. Under incredible heat and pressure the neutron star's hydrogen and helium fused into our series of elements, finally exploding in a super nova that spread the matter of these elements across the universe and with gravity, forming our suns and planets.

These patterns of energy (distributive agents) began to associate according to a rule system that is an artifact of their evolution. Thus began the evolution of subatomic particles and later atomic particles, and later what we call the elements. We now find that the mathematics behind these sub-atomic theories is limited by the assumption of a continuous pattern of smaller and smaller particles. Superstring theory extends the math beyond the limitations of particles and suggests that the math of these primordial string-like patterns of energy completes the Unified Field Theory that ties together Newtonian physics, quantum physics and the general theory of relativity. Bosons, the smallest particles found to date, may represent the limit of science as economics may prevent technology from creating systems for measurement of a smaller class of particles if mathematics is found to suggest such particles.

Ten billion years of increasing complexity of matter led to life. Four more billion years of increasing complexity led to humanity and mind. We have passed through a time of evolution of matter into a time of evolution of mind characterized by explosive information and diminishing time to adapt. Can we imagine even the next thousand years of increasing complexity of mind?

CHAPTER XVII

SO WHAT

As sentient beings, we might speculate that the evolutionary galactic process is an intended consequence, or perhaps an unintended consequence. Even at this level, we struggle with the possibility of a sentient vs. an insentient happening. We sense a rule system whereby evolution takes place and we are divided between a God-start and a non-God-start, and even whether the rule system might be recognized as God. Finally, there is the thought that the concept of God is an unintended consequence of the evolution of mind. Does God exist as thought? Do the acts of people aware of God and his rule-set become his existence? Are these phenomena, in effect and fact, God? Are we then all children of God because we perform God-like acts? We are known by our acts. If we follow the teachings of Jesus and do Jesus' works, then Jesus is known through us. Does God then live through us?

The concept of God, or gods, developed long before our rudimentary understanding of nature. We have inherited a view of God as magical, who said, "Let there be", and it happened. This now seems incomprehensible in the face of too many facts, and much of our religion becomes too brittle to survive. "Only believe" becomes the mantra. Given the system complexity of our universe, it is most likely to be the practical course of action. Occam's razor suggests that the simplest solution is likely to be the right one.

Diversity is an artifact of evolution. Some of us have the capacity to believe. Some do not. Central to this dichotomy is the bulk of the population who struggle with both aspects and are susceptible to either or both views, belief or disbelief. A large part of this group lives in an environment where a belief is forced upon them. Then, there is a penalty for unbelief, or wrong belief. It does not need to be a theocratic society. It can also be a capitalistic society where the creeds of belief are in conflict with societal definitions of need and accomplishment. We find non-belief can be a successful responsibility avoidance strategy, particularly among the more affluent groups. "Religion is the opiate of the masses". "Let them eat cake." "The jobless are too lazy to get jobs."

Scientists believe their profession is one of searching for truth. Truth to them is what can be measured, proven. The rule systems they discover are their truth. They will consider what they can postulate as a theory. Beyond this, the universe is unreal until proven true. What is known is in conflict with what is unknown. The nature of man's mind is such that it tends to block out what does not link with existing knowledge. Is it conceivable that our universe is too complex for us to understand at man's current level of evolution? Is God knowable? Certainly, we cannot prove he exists. It seems arrogant to say that he doesn't exist because we do not have the ability to prove his existence. It is interesting that many of us can be comfortable with the idea of a God particle and super strings, but not with the idea of God. Perhaps we need to apply to God and consciousness the same mathematical zeal that we use to attack super string theory.

If God created man for God's purpose, the natural rule systems, including mathematics, are his rule systems. Evolution is his creation tool. Diversity is an essential part of his creation. It seems unreasonable that his desire is for man to eliminate him or her self. It is simplistic to suggest that he micromanages his works in progress. He did this or that to this or that individual. An unintended consequence of his system might be man's extinction. If free will is the essential freedom required by complexity theory, we might yet destroy ourselves. It seems arrogant for humanity to think that they represent the apex of God's creation process.

An aspect of diversity is that it describes a range or distribution of attributes. From a physical view, we get large vs. small, light vs. dark, etc. From a social view we also get good vs. bad, humble vs. arrogant, etc. We might consider that diversity is the price that we must pay for the only workable creation system. "Bad happens". God does not will it. God suffers it as a result of his system choice. We are the distributive agents in His System. We individually and collectively create his actions. God works through us. We are at the affect of God's/our systems.

Human and much of natural tragedy are sourced in our free will. We speculate that God has some good but unknowable reason for allowing tragic happenings. If we believe in God, we must know that he cares for us. It seems equally possible that God created this self-organizing complex system, but is forced to accept that it lives by its system rules. We might have to loosen up and not expect God to micromanage an inconceivably complex system. Must God be entirely magical? That seems to be a rather human point of view. Perhaps Jesus not only allowed man to sense God, but God to sense man. We no doubt project too much of man's expectations into our sense of God. Is it coincidence that God seems to be struggling with prototypical man in much of the *Old Testament*, before arriving at his *New Testament* strategy? Perhaps God must abide by the creation rule system that is the optimum choice for his purpose.

It makes abundant sense that those actions that further the well-being of mankind as well as each individual are coincident with Christ's teaching. In this sense, we are all children of God when we follow such teaching. It is just as logical to conclude that the discoveries of science prove that God exists, as it proves that he does not exist. We might conclude that the theory of God's existence can be taken as true until proven untrue. God's system is too complex to be knowable, or to be couched in theory. Can we assume that man is an intended consequence of God's system, rather than an unintended consequence? Why Not?

In thinking about complexity theory and religion as a complex system, it would seem that there is a natural dilemma. We tend to think of religion as a stable (read unchangeable) social endeavor. As a social institution and complex system, it should seek to balance on the edge of chaos, between tradition and new. Too much of either leads to extinction. Traditional churches are doubly troubled because the overemphasis on tradition results in loss of members in today's culture. To correct this imbalance, there is a tendency to abandon the traditional rule system, bringing change too fast. Again, it is not change that endangers; it is the rate of change that endangers. This seems consistent with the comment that it is easier to start a new church than to rejuvenate an old one.

Very few people sit around and ponder complexity theory. Fewer yet would see it as a subject for religious thought. Personally, I find nothing to invalidate my belief in God in science. Rather, it seems to me to support his presence. I conclude that belief and disbelief are neuroscience in action. It is said that the first decision that a newborn child must make is whether his or her world is a safe or an unsafe world (the Glass half full or half empty metaphor). There is much need, but often little fertile ground for spiritual growth in an unsafe world. Rather, it is a place where the only recourse is survival, often in the name of religion. For most of us (not all), empathy for the unfortunate that travel with us must begin in the safety of a balanced, loving home. Are we not then left with the insight to love one another? Given the way the system works, this insight is not equally available. Opportunity is also diverse.

The nature of evolution and resulting diversity suggest that blame and judgment should be irrelevant. We all come from the same creation process. We need to look into ourselves before we attempt to see into others. It seems that love and forgiveness are essential to redress any imbalance in creation. If statistical distributions are the rule through natural diversity, distribution from good to evil is inherent in God's system. Then, it is essential for positive agents to act in ways that maintain balance, or better, skew the distribution toward good. This is what we are about as Christians. I believe that this responsibility is best communicated to us in the teachings of Jesus.

CHAPTER XVIII

GOD AND MIND

We think of evolution as a process creating ever increasingly complex systems, the human brain being the most complex living system in the universe. Evolution is a process that provides diversity through which naturally selected species survive. Through adaptation, naturally selected complex systems survive and increase in complexity. Complex systems have a tendency to exhibit properties that are not expressed in the lesser agents that make up the greater systems. We might think of mind in this context

If the human brain is the most complex living system in the universe (as we know it), what is the next level of structure… Mind? Fritjof Capra, observing the layered structure of living systems, suggested that Mind might be a system within the greater systems leading to cosmic Mind, the Mind of God. From the systems view, mind might be thought of as an unintended consequence of system complexity. Living systems self-organize in stratified layers: cells to tissues, tissues to organs, etc. Is mind a new and separate branching of brain? Are there non-physical as well as physical layered structures? Structure is the result of underlying process of self-organization. It is thought, or perhaps, hoped that complexity has the property of convergence.

Living systems not only increase in complexity, but also revert to lesser complexity or push out as new budding systems when the parent system cannot adapt. The evolution of mind might be seen as a new budding system, different from, but in relation to brain. We get the odd image of God re- creating his self: "Abide in me, and I in you. As the branch cannot bear fruit of itself, except it abide in the vine; no more can ye, except ye abide in me." The *Bible* suggests that God created man in his own image. Is God then the Cosmic Self? Is Mind then a lesser system in the greater system of God?

We often find ourselves in a state of surprise and wonder at the many ways in which the energy and matter in our universe exists in a profusion of layers, each layer in relationship with adjacent layers, often in mathematical relationship. The evolution of living systems provides open, self-organizing, self-creating systems of growing complexity. Closed systems devolve, wear out. We have been graced with an environment having an abundance of the requirements for life. In the past century we have reached a population and culture that has made it clear that that abundance is no longer secure. Complex systems that can no longer provide the requirements for increasing complexity, must either become extinct, or revert to a lesser complexity that fits its environment. We get both glimpses of God and of our own limitations. We come to an understanding that we are both a physical being, and a non- physical essence. We have chosen to call the physical being 'real' and the non-physical essence 'unreal'. We also understand that we have mind. We are aware that mind relates to consciousness, but find no concise definition of either. We come to know people by their behavior. We have learned that behavior is a projection of our stored learning, representing the sum of our experiences and some genetic susceptibility. In other words, what we know is who we are, and what we do is who we are. Our personal identity is relatively complete by the age of 5 or 6 years, but we continue to store learning during the rest of our lives. This is reflected in some level of change in behavior over time.

Because our experiences are diverse, both good and bad, we become a mixed bag of both good and bad behavior. To fit the expectation of normality, we are encouraged to strive for a generally positive behavior. We do not have much chance of avoiding some level of negative traits, and so we are introduced to the idea of discipline and the work of learning to become socially acceptable. That is to minimize self-defeating traits.

Faith is said to be instinctive. Faith is not belief, but offers the potential for belief. Belief is learned. Faith comes before belief. Faith supports belief. We are challenged to become Christians. Since belief is learned, we must do the work of learning to become Christian. A Christian is a person who has made a passionate commitment to pursue the teachings of Jesus. The first step is the work of reaching belief through faith. The second step is the work of following Jesus' teaching. For most of us, this is a best effort situation. We are not all saints.

Each of us comes to religion with our own unique identity. We each have our own level of skills and abilities, our own level of education, our own social and financial status. The idea is to create in your mind a quality image of a passionate commitment to Jesus. Your works will then be defined by that belief. The meaning in your life will be in relationship to your own expectations and perceptions, to the history of good and bad choices that you have made.

As humans, we have a mind that is inquisitive, creative, and logical. As we read the *Bible*, we cannot help trying to imagine God and Jesus. We have considered one view of God as a cosmic Mind, sitting at the top of a universal living system. Neither neuroscience, nor systems theory existed when the *Bible* stories and documents were created. We have so much more information now to facilitate interpretation of what we experience. *The Gospel of John* is preeminent in presenting Jesus as God. As we read *The Gospel of John*, his presentation of Jesus' words seem to fit a god-mind metaphor. Is God of Mind? Is God in Mind? Is God Mind? Does God exist? Is God real? Can we approach these questions with the wisdom of participation in God's creation, with some understanding of way the world works? Following are some examples:

> "In the beginning was the word, and the word was with God, and the word was God."

John refers to Jesus as the word and to the word as God. In the language of the Bible, words and thoughts have equal power. Jesus' teaching defines who he is. Jesus teaches belief in God. To John, Jesus and God are one.

"God is spirit and he that worships him must worship him in spirit and in truth." God is not physical. Is he then not real? How do we worship in spirit? Mind is not physical. Is Mind spirit? We worship him through Mind, and through mind project him in our behavior that is real.

"He that hear my word, and believe on him that sent me, have everlasting life." What is Jesus' word... his teaching... belief in God? Those who believe in Jesus do the Father's works.

"And ye have not his word abiding in you; for whom he hath sent, him ye believe not." If you do not believe in Jesus, you do not believe in God. God's word is belief in Jesus. God and Jesus are one through belief.

"This is the work of God that ye believe on him whom he hath sent." Belief in Jesus is the work of God.

"Therefore I say unto you, that no man can come unto me, except it be given unto him of my Father." It is through belief in God that man finds belief in Jesus. Belief in Jesus must be obtained through belief in God.

"If ye continue in my word, then are ye my disciples indeed." "If a man keeps my saying, he shall never see death." "I and my Father are one."

"Though ye believe not me, believe the works: that ye may know, and believe, that the Father is in me, and I in him."

"Believe me that I am in the Father and the Father in me, or else believe me for the very work's sake."

"If a man loves me, he will keep my words: and my Father will love him, and we will come unto him and make our abode with him."

"This is my commandment, that ye love one another, as I have loved you."

How do we interpret these writings, given the freedom to use what we know as citizens of the 21st Century? We are told that God is spirit. To worship God we must worship him in spirit. Can we worship God in spirit and not ourselves be spirit? Is it possible for Jesus to be in God and God in Jesus other than in spirit? All of our religious practices are or are in support of mental constructs. Perhaps, spirit and mind are one in the context of religion. That is, God and Jesus are one in the context of mind. You see God in the works of Jesus, not in Jesus' physical body. God's intent, his works are that we believe in Jesus. In belief we are give the ability to create the spiritual realm. We are made in the image of God. Might this suggest that God, Jesus and man share capacity for spiritual awareness? Prayer supports belief. If through belief in Jesus we do God's work, do we not live beyond physical death in our works? If through our works we further God's purpose, can we not recognize that this is sufficient?

Chapter XIX

God's Purpose

The Bible says that before the world began, God was. Given that man's awareness of God began when man's complexity evolved to a level to exhibit mind, it is likely that the idea of God existing before the world began was symbolic exaltation. It is difficult to imagine God waiting 14 billion years for man to arrive at a level where such awareness was possible, even though we assume that the God we worship is not bounded by time and space.

On the other hand, if we need our God to exist before the world began, we can think of the God we know as infinite where as man is finite. We have no language to image God's infinite domain. Perhaps God existed in his domain before the Big Bang occurred in our world. Perhaps, he pulled the trigger. Then, the evolution of man's brain to a level that exhibits mind provided a doorway between God's domain and our world. God in our world exists and acts through us. Our belief invites Him into our life. Our belief makes God real in our world through our behavior.

Through mind, man became self-aware and came into communication with God. Thus, man became aware of his universe and his position in the universe. That is, man's physical limitations of time and space. For man, then, God came into existence with man's self-awareness, probably initially as a survival mechanism and with many different gods.

Through mind and with the need for God, man came into communication with God. Man then became aware of God's purpose for man. Jesus stated that that purpose is for man to love God and to love his neighbor. God's purpose requires that man evolve mind beyond self-preservation, to the level of exhibiting loving relationships as a dominant behavioral characteristic of humanity.

Loving relationships are the key to fulfilling the prime directive of the human system: survival, avoidance of extinction. As living systems, and systems within systems, we must survive to maintain the self and transcend the self to a state of loving relationships.

To evolve to the level of loving relationships we must bring our intellectual mind in balance with our emotional mind. We cannot remain in a state where relatively small portions of humanity can access the results of our combined intellectual efforts with the intent to exert power over large portions of humanity. Such behaviors breed conflict and are exhausting the natural resources by which we survive.

It becomes obvious that God's purpose for humanity and humanities purpose for humanity are one and the same. If humanity is one of God's living systems, then it is logical that that system should be in harmony with God's purpose. If humanity continues to express behaviors that threaten the survival of the earth's ecosystem, humanity will become extinct, or be forced backward to an earlier level of cultural complexity. Will a step backward to a time of less complexity offer a step forward toward God's purpose? It has happened before with extinction events.

Christianity is the primary religion of the world's privileged classes. Yet, modern Christianity is likely to lose 80% of that membership over the next few decades. How is this loss of Christian ethics impacting our world? The leadership of the privileged class has been a key contributor to every major war and financial crisis. Today's financial crisis is the greatest since the stock market began. It has squandered trillions of dollars and put the entire world in crisis. Pensions are gone. 401Ks are empty. Life savings have disappeared. Jobs are gone. Companies are downsizing and entering bankruptcy.

Churches are closing. The thousands of people that survive on the charity of others are now dying of starvation.

Laws have been changed through lobbying to allow high risk investments, supported by institutions we pay to protect our assets. Key members of Government vote to make finance laws more lax and vote against tighter controls. All these institutions and their leaders are paid to protect our interests, but act in their own interest. The result is theft of the savings, jobs, homes, businesses, churches, and lives…. of millions of people that our Government is sworn to protect.

What has this to do with religion? What about Church and State? That separation was written into the Constitution. Were politicians less corrupt at that time? I think not. If our Government can't protect us and our property, who can? Who will? As living systems, governments, political parties, politicians all have their own survival as their prime directive. Their resulting dominant focus is money and power. Never have so few brought so much grief to so many.

What underlies this pervasive self-defeating behavior? Has the world become too complex? Have the natural systems that control normality, homeostasis, been abandoned? Where has our system of checks and balances gone? Systems are in crisis when polarization eliminates the decision process. The far right and far left of our governing body represent small party groups who through the longevity of consecutive terms claim the right and obligation to define their personal party truths as National truths. This control psychology results in the self-defeating behavior, symptomatic of the downward spiral to system death. Never has there been a greater need for a return to a god purpose and an ethic of intrinsic rightness.

CHAPTER XX

RELIGION AND ETHICS

Can you be a good person without being religious? The answer is yes. Every culture has a value system. These systems are about moral duty and about ideal behavior. Moral duty and ideal behavior are defined by that particular culture. Is there a moral duty and ideal character that spans all cultures? This is the intent of religion, but religions, as complex living systems, are susceptible to the diversity of human behavior. Illogical self- defeating behavior is a fact of life in any group. This sets up a dynamic of good and bad behavior that is the territory of moral duty and ideal behavior. This is also the territory of religion.

Ethics is the branch of philosophy that deals with right and wrong, good and bad. Ethics is the science of morals and morals are the practice of ethics. In this sense, a good person is an ethical person, moral and with ideal behavior. Early religions are about control and growth, or growth and control. The startup energy required to obtain growth is motivated by controlling leadership. Liberalism and freedom come later, along with stability.

Religion includes a particular idea about ethical behavior. That is the belief that there is an intrinsic rightness that defines moral duty and ideal behavior. This involves belief in and worship of a righteous god head. It also involves the respect and love of fellow humans, Jesus' 2nd

Commandment. If we are successful in these requirements, we will be successful in obeying the law, the Ten Commandments, by default.

Our attempts to form utopian societies have failed miserably because of an intolerable diversity among the participants. The understanding of rules of good behavior does not confer the ability to practice them. The central tendency in the distribution of behavior is a mix of both positive and negative behavior. To assemble a group of people directed at a particular mission requires a leader who can motivate a net positive behavior. It is impractical to dictate behavior without eliminating freedom and choice. The alternative is to be selective in who can belong to the group. These considerations make the idea of an ethic of intrinsic rightness difficult to apply. Intrinsic rightness is not measurable.

People responsible for large groups, corporations, governments, are drawn to an ethic that is measureable. Universalism is such an ethic. The mechanism is a set of rules that define the actions of the group. Measurement defines the nature of the impact of the rules and actions on the members of the group. The actions have more or less utility in providing a positive experience to group members. There are two types of this ethic: 1) the action makes most members better off, with no one less well off (Pareto Efficiency), 2) the action makes most members better off, with some members worse off (Kaldor-Hicks Efficiency). These ethics allow statistical measurement. These ethics are labeled consequentialism, an ethic of results. In practice, Kaldor-Hicks efficiency can operate as Pareto Efficiency if through some process of distribution additional wealth or utility can be transferred from the haves to the have-nots such that no one is left worse off.

The ethics of religion are called deontological, pressuring for intrinsic rightness. The ethics of universalism are called teleological, an ethic of results. The ethic of results leaves governments with the problem of creating a stable balance between haves and have-nots. The task is to take enough from the haves to avoid revolution by the have-nots. This sort of revolution has been a common occurrence throughout history. For democracies, the have-nots through population size ultimately control the votes, leading to the destruction of the economy and leading to a cyclical rise and fall in government.

The obvious position of churches in this process is to create pressure for a stable balance in the distribution of wealth based on their ethic of intrinsic rightness. Wealth and power corrupts. Where else is there dedication to a counterbalance? The wealthy tend to corrupt the government. The government writes laws for their own survival and growth. Political parties, as complex living systems, live by the same system rules for survival. The result is a formula for the natural rise and fall of democratic societies. Given this awareness, one would think that the cycle can be avoided. The problem is the natural diversity of human behavior. Illogical self-defeating behavior is alive and well in any society. It seems that we are not yet evolved enough as a society to find a practical balance between the ethic of universalism and the ethic of intrinsic rightness.

For the past 10 years or so, there has been great emphasis on Globalization. The modern corporations and thus their governments pursue globalization to spread democracy and free market ideas around the world. Bigger is better. Deregulation is better. The mathematical logic is obvious. What is also obvious, but ignored is that human nature is involved. You cannot apply science and mathematics without consideration of human nature. The Club of Rome and their Operations Research Project was a classic example. Also, it has been shown that cooperation suffers in direct relation to the physical distance between the parties. How do third world countries protect themselves against the intrusion of first world ideas that are irrelevant to their evolutionary status?

The destabilizing activity of world corporations, the IMF and the World Bank in developing countries is legendary. Time is critical in the evolutionary process. What took the developed world 500 years to accomplish, we are suggesting the developing world accomplish in 30 years and to whose advantage? Who is a major advocate for the developing world, calling for elimination of slavery through debt… church organizations? In most fields of endeavor it is the church that acts to pressure for balance, life- enhancing behavior, and the minimization (regulation) of the greed and control psychology inherent in complex living systems.

CHAPTER XXI

THE RIVER

India is known for its belief in sacred rivers. My journey in discussing how the world works has had me looking for simulations that might help envision my thoughts. What has come up is the vision of a river. This is partly due to my feeling that God's purpose for man involves an ongoing evolutionary process. As complex living systems, some of us believe that human evolution has the property of convergence. Our lives are not random, but are moving toward an end that is God's purpose for us. We, however, are each in our particular time and space in this continuum and our time is limited. Our potential is to contribute to the process and the convergence. It is most unlikely that we will participate in an ending. We do the best we can in the time we are allotted.

A continuum is like a river. We might think of the water as faith, a potential to believe. Belief, itself, is learned. It comes after faith and may be understood as built on that faith potential. In this analogy, we float along on the current of faith, building our unique identity as we experience life on the river. Given our diversity of experience, we may be swimming down stream, across the stream, or even upstream. Down stream is the way the world works. We are agents in this flowing continuum moving toward God's purpose.

Clearly, we ought to be swimming down stream. In spite of our diversity, what is true is that we are all on this river together.

Ideally, we would all swim downstream as fast as possible, reducing the time for the accomplishment of God's intent. The nature of evolution and diversity is such that we are a population with potential for both the logical and the illogical, in a rather unstable balance. We are shown the way to abundant life, but our diversity of good and bad behavior places us in a tug of war both for and against such life. Since for most of us the basis for our beliefs is forged early in life, we find the battlefield often encompasses the very young. The generation in power has the opportunity to imprint the young with their particular vision, perpetuating paradigms that can be adverse, if not perverse, to God's purpose.

We move through our time spending it as though there were no ending. The daily decisions that make the history of our lives are chaotic with little sense of direction or meaning. The great opportunity we are given to be a part of God's purpose for us slips away like sand through our fingers. It is nearness of death that asks us for an accounting, and for meaning. God need not judge. We judge ourselves. It is an act of love to help our brothers and sisters to become aware and search for meaning, so that they can value themselves. In the end, there is little quite as comforting as a life well spent, a life given meaning.

CHAPTER XXII

Consciousness

We humans have consciousness. It is yet to be defined; perhaps it cannot be 'defined', as its contexts are multiple. Consciousness is a construct of mind and therefore is defined as unreal, not measurable. Consciousness is about awareness, awareness of self. It is said that 95 percent of the Mind is unconscious and 5 percent conscious. Is the unconscious mind aware… apparently? We seem to have instinctive awareness and conscious awareness. We might think of conscious awareness as self-reflective mental life.

Psychiatrists delve into unconsciousness to expose the traumatic experiences that are the basis for mental constructs that cause unhealthy behavior. Their intervention includes drugs, hypnosis, word association, etc. For therapists, consciousness is irrelevant and for some, non-existent. For therapists, behavior is real. They analyze illogical behavior to expose the "I must" and "I demand" core beliefs that project illogical behavior. Successful intervention provides a new awareness directed at behavioral change.

Religion is in the awkward position of straddling the gap between science and psychology. Religion has its residence in Mind, but must practice its profession in the physical world. They hope for spiritual growth that increases self-esteem and that is projected as love. It must utilize psychology while not perceived as doing so.

Its members populate the 85% that represent the central behavioral tendency in a normal distribution.

Mystical (Eastern) View:

Consciousness is primary, the ground of all being and the essence of living beings. Pure consciousness, or cosmic consciousness, has certain patterns. Some of these patterns are matter. In other words, all the matter in the universe arises out of consciousness.

Scientific (Western) View:

Consciousness is a phenomenon that emerges out of matter at some high level of complexity. Complexity results from continued successful adaptation to environmental change. All structure is the result of underlying process, the process of self-organization. Consciousness is a phenomenon of mind. Mind is the essence of self-organization (Capra).

Synthesis:

Consciousness is an attribute of Mind. Consciousness, the essence of all living beings, has certain patterns, some of which are non-material essence. This is similar to the sub-atomic particles, the fermions that make up all the matter in the universe and bosons that are the smallest particles and have no material properties. We have a non-physical entity we call Mind with the attribute of consciousness that gives us awareness of both matter and essence, awareness of self and others, awareness of our environment. Consciousness gives us the opportunity for relationships, some which are instinctive and some which we choose.

If we presume that Mind has a layered structure of systems within systems, we then might expect a planetary mind, a galactic mind and a cosmic mind to exist. In this sense, the cosmic consciousness and the cosmic mind are one and the same system, the preeminent level of which we call God.

In the beginning was God, consciousness. God created the Universe. Through evolution, God created Man, and with Man,

Mind. Man has awareness of God, and through God, of self. God has physical presence in the works of Man. Man seeks God by transcending self, pursuing the works of Jesus.

In the Eastern View, we see man traveling through several lifetimes, each life attempting to manage his or her behavior in ways that will allow progression toward the highest level of consciousness, Nirvana. Reaching Nirvana allows escape from this world of suffering.

In the Western View, we see man traveling through one lifetime, attempting to model his or her behavior according to the teaching of Jesus, to win a place in God's "Kingdom" in an afterlife.

The intent is to contribute to the fulfillment of God's purpose for mankind (Thy will be done.) The concepts of Heaven and Hell are motivational tools, a part of resurrection theology, accepted as literal by some and symbolic by others. Both the Eastern and Western views advocate a positive life experience with convergence toward a pure consciousness that many think of as God.

Purification is the process of emptying one's self of self-defeating behaviors that limit abundant life on earth and prepares us for an afterlife. The process of emptying requires significant effort that is, in effect, immersion in a self-transcending idea such as Jesus' teaching of love. We find the common theme of a life well lived, and an either/or duality at death: to win a next life, or to win our way out of a next life. There is no end to diversity in human thought. It would seem wise to choose to live a life with meaning, just in case. Christianity has been the popular choice to date.

Chapter XXIII

Illusion and Reality

Some existentialists have the nihilistic view that existence is all illusion. This suggests that nothing is simply nothing. When is nothing simply nothing? Perhaps illusion is something, even something profound. It has been proposed for over 2000 years that the world might be made of small particles called atoms. In the early 1800s atomic theory was first proposed. It was finally accepted in the 1930s. Quantum theory was initiated at the end of the 19th century and is a center of interest in current physics. Names like superstring theory and zero energy field are used describe the nature of the sub-atomic or quantum landscape.

We have gone from describing the smallest particle of matter to describing the smallest quantity of energy. We can mathematically relate matter to energy. We find that all our particles are patterns of energy, the smallest of which is now call the 'god particle'. Experiments have recently validated its existence. The stratified nature of the universe must end somewhere. We find that our universe is made up of patterns of energy. Nothing is as it appears. Even empty space has properties (it can be bent by gravitation) and is thus something. All is illusion. Yet, all exists. For illusion to exist there must be a complex living system with Mind to create the idea of illusion. Living systems are made up of sub-systems upon sub-systems, all patterns of energy, all following system rules. We are yet to understand what consciousness and Mind are, though we see their impact in the reality of our behavior.

With Mind come the curiosity and the creativity to imagine what might be. If the entire universe is a sea of energy, we can imagine that the ebb and flow of energy creates turbulence and thus vortices that take on shape, perhaps similar to turbulent water flow, and express unique properties. These vortices of energy might express properties like matter and experience attractive forces. We can then imagine all sorts of patterns growing out of this primordial sea of energy.

We have come from defining this energy as particle-like to the limits of particle mathematics and are now drawn into superstring theory that extends our mathematical journey toward the infinitely small. We are faced with existentialist questions of who and why. Is this sea of energy a puddle formed on a rainy night in another dimension, or the creation of a sentient being in that dimension, and if so, to what purpose? The ideas about God are always ideas about the unknown. Are we a creation or a random event?

We are now challenged with the mathematics of superstring theory and dark matter. Is our puddle of energy composed of fiber-like loops as the logic of math allows? If dark energy and dark matter represents 95 % of what makes up the universe, then all that we observe and measure represents the other 5%. Then, perhaps the Big Bang was a trivial happening in the greater universe of matter and energy. Living systems make up an infinitely small part of the 5% of knowable matter. Still only the human component of living systems has a brain that has evolved to exhibit Mind and contemplate God.

We have come to understand some about how the brain works to create mind through neuroscience and observations of behavior. We can scan the brain with MRI and see how sensory input changes blood flow in some of the 800 brain parts. We have discerned experientially how the brain learns. We know there is a genetic component to personality development, but we don't know whether it is DNA or experience that is dominant in our personality development. Perhaps one or the other, or a balance is irrelevant. We would like to think that experience is a large component of learning because it gives us hope that changing negative learning might be practical. What becomes obvious is that diversity of all systems and processes in nature impact all of existence, including our learning and our sense of self.

Diversity is an essential feature in the process of evolution. Diversity provides the options for natural selection. Systems survive as a result of their ability to adapt to their changing environment. In the diversity of options, Nature selects those whose attributes support change. When we consider an issue like genetics vs. eugenics of behavior, we soon realize that diversity makes dominance obscure. We look at the statistics to form some acceptable picture that we might call 'normal'. This convention allows us to select who can belong and who cannot. It is obvious that there must be some boundaries for acceptable behavior for the survival of a primary system.

What Nature will not tolerate is equality. Yet, driven to seek moral rightness, we find this theme in many areas of human endeavor. Equality requires the elimination of options. The freedom to choose, that is so fundamental that it mirrors the nature of evolution, becomes a primary target for living systems which seek domination over lesser systems. The primary directive of all living systems to survive leads to a pervasive attitude of domination and growth. This same path which is a successful strategy for embryonic systems is the path of extinction for old systems. The idea of a balanced, mature system seems an anathema. Almost all systems pass into extinction as their webs of relationships become rigid, limiting the information required for timely change. The vision of a mature, eternal system is illusory as the success of that system breeds a failure to remember how that success was attained.

Since the human mind is the most complex living system in our universe, we sense that there must be a convergence to our existence that we think of as our purpose for being. Whether our existence is the result of an unintended event in a complex system, or the plan of a sentient life form beyond our comprehension, we are the result: a complex living system evolved to the level to exhibit Mind. To date, we sit at the top of the evolutionary pyramid in the context of self-awareness, logic and creativity. When we speak of illusion, we are drawn into the duality of real vs. unreal. This discussion only occurs because its perspective is based on what we experience vs. what we can imagine or think of. Illusion is a matter of context. In the context of the physical world, objects are real. In the context of Mind, mental objects are real. In both contexts they exist, but they are real only in their own context.

Given the way our brain works to store learning, we have some control over the processes of learning. We can feed the mind through the repetition of rote learning. We learn the math tables. We learn vocabulary. These become the database for more complex thought. When we create a new idea or understanding, it is through relational pathways between previous thoughts and ideas. These resulting new ideas also becomes part of our database of stored learning. Through higher levels of thought we not only function to gain understanding, but also to gain the skill and ability for even higher thought.

What we have learned about learning is that our mind can create and make real for us, in the inner world of mind, whatever we are willing to spend the time and effort required for that learning. This is an immersion process. We can learn to play the piano if we are willing to spend the years required to learn and with a positive attitude toward learning. We have a magnificent creative mind. We confuse lack of ability with lack of motivation. Of course, it is not an equal opportunity process. Nature is diverse in all its processes. The brain has far more capacity for learning than anyone will ever use. In fact, in your teenage years, the Mind will eliminate half your neurons, the ones that you don't use. That will still leave you with about 500 billion, enough to keep you learning, albeit at a some what slower rate. The point is that you can create for yourself any way of being, any reality that you choose. It is a matter if immersing yourself in whatever great idea that you choose. Can you imagine it? You have to think with awe on what God has created.

Because our learning system stores both positive and negative experiences, we wind up with a mixed bag of life-enhancing and life-defeating behavior as expressed by that stored learning. The way the brain stores learning makes it easier to process information that it has already received. The pathways become less resistant as the same or similar information is processed. This gives us preference for previously stored information. Confirmation of what we already know gives us pleasure. What we know is who we are. What we do is who we are. We are known by our works. Change threatens who we are. Thus, change is pain. This process protects our unique identity, but also puts a spin on how we see the world. We tend to protect our self-defeating behavior the same as we protect our self-enhancing behavior. The tantrum that is effective as a child in reducing stress becomes a coping behavior that, through repetition, is carried into adulthood with self-defeating results.

Nihilism is a self-defeating philosophy of existence that sees the world as absurd and without purpose. It sees the world as an illusion. This is a path that leads toward authoritative, intellectualizing, and antisocial behavior. Self-defeating behavior limits or eliminates positive relationships. Since human beings are relational beings, life is a struggle to balance ones self- enhancing and self-defeating behaviors.

Fundamental in Nature are freedom and choosing. Even the evolutionary process operates by creating diversity, the availability of choice, and selection, the chosen path for adaptation. Individually, we are faced with a flood of events in our lives and are faced with the need to choose our responses. We agree that choosing positive relationships is correct, but our self-defeating behaviors inhibit correct choices. We are often driven to choose negative relationships to validate our self-defeating behavior. Our survival instinct overrides logic. We protect who we are, good or bad.

Consciously or unconsciously, we always choose. We are driven to belong in seeking self-esteem. Consciously or unconsciously we choose a life- enhancing or a life-defeating existence. We will choose an existence that reflects our stored learning, be that good or bad. Where is the freedom in this? Low self-esteem limits freedom of choice. The issue becomes one of awareness. Freedom comes with change. Change comes with the hope for change and a supportive environment that encourages adaptation. The objective is enlightened self-esteem.

Given the freedom and choice, would you prefer to remain in your present state or minimize your self-defeating behavior. Given freedom and opportunity would you choose to believe in a creator God, or a random event? Would you choose to believe that life is an illusion, or a reality? If you could make a benevolent God real for you, would you make the effort? Most Americans say that they are Christians. This often means that they are aware of Christianity, having spent some time in the past in church or with Christians. It may mean they go to church every Sunday. To be a Christian requires us to express Jesus' teaching in our behavior and works. This requires us to immerse ourselves to the extent that we are known by others as Christians. We are seen to walk the walk. It requires us to do the work of minimizing our self-defeating behavior.

Because we each have different skills and abilities and different experiences, we each respond differently to the events in our lives. We each have a different perspective on religion and on God. How we respond is hugely influenced by our earliest experiences at church and with learning. There is always a gap between how we behave and how we know that we should behave. This gap is increased when we think about how we behave vs. how Jesus taught us to behave. This is tied up in our mix of good and bad learning. Knowing how to behave is not a cure for bad behavior. Our behavior, good and bad, is the result of habituation from years of repetition.

Limiting or eliminating bad behavior requires purging the mind with positive behavior. Neurons respond to the use it or lose it principle. Neurons also respond to the no pain, no gain principle. Effort at the level of immersion in positive behavior is required. These mental processes are the same for any unlearning and relearning in any discipline whether playing the piano or becoming a Christian. We suffer from the illusion that we cannot change. Illusion is a cage that we place ourselves in through the lack of commitment to change negative behavior. The bars of the cage get stronger with the repetition of negative thoughts until it becomes real for us.

CHAPTER XXIV

SCIENCE VS. MIND

Science has been said to be a search for truth. Scientists are human beings. History is full of incidences of science used to circumvent truth. Disproven theories become untruths, yet are so hard to change that new truths become heresy.

Phillip Semmelweis developed antiseptic surgery 100 years before Lister. He noted that women giving birth were dying from puerperal fever. He realized that this was due to doctors going from autopsies to birthing, bringing something on their unclean hands. Women at term were hiding rather than going to lying-in hospitals where so many died. Dr. Semmelweis significantly cut the rate of deaths in his hospital by washing his hands with lime water. He was ridiculed, hounded from his profession and died a pauper for insisting that doctors should wash their hands before deliveries. Such activity was thought to disgrace and degrade his profession. Puerperal fever was obviously unpreventable in his time. Darwin's *Origin of the Species* caused so much conflict, given biblical logic over that period that it was not widely accepted as a theory for 80 years after it was first written. It is clear from the history of science that scientists are very resistant to new information. This might be considered a form of narcissism, obsessive self-esteem.

Prior to Galileo's house arrest for continuing his support of Copernicus's theory that the earth revolves around the sun, a monk was burned at the stake for that heresy. The Church as a living system was responding to its primary imperative of survival. The world *must* work according to church biblical logic. Beware of musts and demands in your core beliefs! We have to ask, "What in the world is this all about?" People were required not to see what they saw, not to hear what they heard. It is certainly not about the science. It is about how people learn, develop their identity, and project their behavior: the fact of stories becoming false truths, of herding instinct, of the need to belong. With logic on overload, science became separate from religion,

It took until the 20th Century for scientists to admit that there are natural phenomena that can't be measured, but that are so obvious in their cyclical patterns that they can be theorized and accepted as science. This is "comparative science" and includes theories such as general systems theory, complexity theory, chaos theory, etc. These sciences are also involved in the search for truth about the way the world works.

We have used these theories to talk about the way the world works, and about whether these theories might give us new insights into our religious belief. If we believe that God is the Creator, then these systems and systems within systems are his systems. If God has a purpose for mankind, these systems are fulfilling that purpose. Yet, we see that his systems are not perfect. That is, his systems allow bad as well as good to happen. This ultimately leads us to how the mind works and particularly to our often illogical, self-defeating behavior. This behavior reflects the nature of our learning system and accounts for most of humanity's problems.

Given the rate of genetic change we should expect no substantive change in the brain, but we can make substantive changes in how we manage the information that feeds it, and thus in our mind and resultant behavior. We know that the dendrites, the hair like fingers at the receiving end of our neurons, move closer together with reception of like or similar information. We know that these pathways decay with disuse. This changes the brain and supports the memory, but is not genetic change. This mechanism is functional in the present and is the door to behavioral change. We have the opportunity to open this door to a flood of positive thoughts and experiences.

What of instinct? Are these also evolutionary accomplishments that have preset the brain for specific actions? They are common and likely survival related. Some seem to have decayed through disuse. They are vestigial but some occasionally show up in some degree. Empathy and compassion are the relatively new attributes which represent evolutionary changes in the brain. They are common, but a long way from dominant. The nature's diversity can be subtle. It can be seen in the uneven rates of evolutionary change across large populations and through many generations. This diversity gives us a preview of future possibilities. We find some individuals that currently excel in cerebral behavior, expressing an advanced level of compassion and empathy. Will our culture become more benevolent?

In the time continuum of the world of evolution, creation, science defines its territory as the real world of physics and chemistry bounded by the measurable. The continuum of creation extends backward into the immeasurable infinitely small and forward into the immeasurably complex. While the location of science in the continuum is reasonably well defined, the location of the scientist suffers from his presence in both the domain of science and the domain of the remainder of creation, of mind. The scientist must deal with the fuzzy boundary between vocation, science, and self, mind. The scientist, after all, is a human being. This requires a precise definition of the boundaries of science to avoid intrusion of unreal mental constructs such as expectations and perceptions.

CHAPTER XXV

LESSONS FROM STRING THEORY

Superstring Theory is the mathematics of the quantum world, the world of subatomic particles and empty space. In the 17th century the scientific world of Newton and the mathematics of calculus suggested that everything that could be discovered had been. Physics was said to be complete. In the 20th century, it was said that physics was not complete, but it might be found complete in quantum physics. By complete, physicists meant that they could describe or predict everything in the world. This would include defining consciousness and the residence of God. Regardless of the idea of faith, some mathematicians seem to be searching for a logic that most accept does not exist. To qualify, a theory of God would require a hypothesis that is about 95% proven in the lab. I wouldn't buy stock in it as a theory. Consciousness presents a similar conundrum. What is the elemental stuff of thought, a pattern of energy... a dynamic between multiple patterns of energy?

When physics gets to a level where it no longer has the technology for measurement, physics ends and its companion, mathematics continues on. At that level mathematics is about visualizing a model of what might be and then discovering the mathematics (logic) to validate the model. Mathematics evolves the logic to refine the hypothesis (model). What is exciting about this process is that mathematics can predict outcomes within and beyond our technology Unified field theory suggests a continuum of forces from the cosmos to the quantum world. When the idea of particles could no longer support further research, a new idea was required Thus we have moved from particle physics to string theory. How could particles and vibrating strings be related? Vibrating strings vibrate with wave-like motion. The waves have highs and lows and nodes, like the letter 'S' lying on its side. Nodes are points at the middle and ends of a wave that have no motion. In mathematics, the nodes can take on the properties of particles. The idea of a vibrating string opened the door to new paths for investigation. Interestingly enough, many of the mathematical tools for this accomplishment, vibrating strings, had already been developed.

We sometimes think of God as a resident in another dimension. This is the stuff of Sci-Fi, but also of mathematics. Einstein took Pythagoras Theorem to a new level. That is, the square of the hypotenuse of a triangle equals the sum of the square of the two sides. We visualize the triangle as having a square flag of area extending from each side. If a right triangle has a vertical side that changes length, the sum of the areas attached to the two sides remains constant as area transfers from one side square to the other side square. The sum is still equal to the hypotenuse square area. In mathematics, each of the three sides of a triangle can be treated as a different dimension.

If the bottom end of the hypotenuse is moved sideways a bit, a new area is formed, but the total area of the now three squares of the sides still equal the hypotenuse area and thus Pythagoras Theorem still applies. Einstein let this new side be time, adding a fourth dimension. This is the definition of our universe of three space dimensions and a temporal dimension. From this Einstein developed the theory of relativity relating energy to mass. ($E = MC^2$) This insight teaches that in mathematics there can be as many dimensions as desired by adding more positions to the hypotenuse, creating more sides and giving more areas without changing the hypotenuse area. This has become known as Einstein's hypotenuse.

We occasionally think about God as residing in a different world, a different dimension from our own. I occasionally wonder if Mind is a doorway for communicating with that different dimension, perhaps in prayer. Our world has only three dimensions that we might label as X, Y, & Z in math. Higher math leads to equations defining many different dimensions. Physicists add time as a dimension in describing our world. In string theory, the mathematics allows for 9 dimensions plus time. For these ideas to be real, they must conform to the reality of our physical world. This involved finding the mathematical relationships which would logically reduce the 9 dimensions to the three dimensions plus time of our real world. Ultimately, the ideas about new particles that this mathematics predicts will remain ideas until we find ways to measure them and give them the name 'real'. Mathematics seems to be magical in its ability to predict entities before they can be proven by measurement. If mathematics cannot find a formula to prove God's existence, it can predict any number of other worldly dimensions where God might reside. God's created world is often found to be logically, mathematically consistent and to have the attribute of beauty in its logical construction.

CHAPTER XXVI

Religion

Religion is the sum of Man's thoughts about God. The *Bible* is the early history of Judaism and Christianity. It presents God as Creator. It presents the "word of God" through the *Bible*. Religious denominations vary in their degree of literal interpretation of the *Bible* and in their emphasis on the *Old Testament* vs. *New Testament*. The authority of the *Bible* as Christianity's primary guiding document is not in question. Traditional religions have been losing membership for the past 50 or so years. In the developed world, according to recent surveys, church attendance is motivated more by recreation than by a search for and worship of God. It has been proposed that this is in part due to an inability to reconcile biblical teaching with current science. It is no doubt more complicated than that.

Anyone who thinks seriously about the *Bible* with at least one foot in the 'real' world will realize that 'divinely inspired' begs interpretation. To speak of the *Bible* as inerrant is to make the *Bible* a god, an idol. If humanity along with all of Nature is diverse, including a diversity of unique human identities, then God's intent would seem to be a message clear to all people, however interpreted. We can think of the *Bible* as cut in stone, or as a message that is written so as to be time and culture independent. We should keep in mind that a *Bible* cut in stone eliminates God's gift of freedom and choice. We should also keep in mind that the Ten Commandments were cut in stone and had to be reinterpreted by Jesus. The diverse nature of humanity is such that it cannot live by the law alone, but also through loving relationships. God understands diversity. He created it.

Typical homilies make comparisons between *bible* stories and current experiences, as a means to support biblical belief. The current response seems to be "been there; done that". Resistance seems to involve the utilizing of stories as literal truths, thus placing the *Bible* and religion in doubt. As parents give up church as a part of their lives, we can no longer expect parents to immerse their children in biblical teaching to capture their young minds for a lifetime. Young adults tend to treat church-going as one more way parents seek to control their children. The indoctrinated child population is like fossil fuel. The reservoir is beyond its peak. To add to this problem the typical church family that averaged 3 children in the year 1900 now averages less than 1. If church membership has been dropping for 50 years, so has been the availability of immersed minds. We expect that church membership would include a disproportionate number of seniors.

It is perhaps heretical to suggest that there is too much dependence on the *Bible* in the Christian religion. Yet, there seems to be a sort of disconnect between the biblical idea of God as Creator, and God's creation. The *Bible* suggests that you can know God through the works of Jesus. Can we know God by observing God's creation… the works of God? From the quantum world to the cosmos, God's creation is awesome. Knowing is the work of Mind. Man has the most complex living system in the known universe, the human brain. Through Mind, man became aware of the need for god, and then evolved to communicate with God. Jesus brings a reality to that communication.

We accept the idea of God through faith, the proposition that there are truths which cannot be proven by evidence or logic. God is infinite and beyond understanding. It is in the nature of our creative mind that we imagine God. It is natural that we personalize God to add a sense of reality to what is spiritual, unreal. Real is defined as what is measurable. Ideas, thoughts, quality, feelings, as mental constructs, are unreal. Mental constructs exist, but are defined as unreal. Since science is real and religion is unreal, the two are separated by their naming. Which has more relevance? Which is more motivating, 'real' or 'unreal'? When searching for an understanding of their relationship with the idea of God, both scientist and theologian realize their expectations. They are likely to find their God (or not) in their own expectations, not in science or theology.

If God is Creator, then evolution is the creation tool. Since evolution is based on selection from a diverse population of choices, diversity is a requirement for life. This selection process supports those options that are most adaptable to the changing environment. It has become clear that genetic change is small nearly to the level of stasis. Sudden change in environment (punctuated equilibrium) accelerates evolution by eliminating established species and shifting nature back to life forms that are more adaptable. This punctuated equilibrium seems to fit the fossil record. Perhaps adaptation rate presents a more relevant aspect in the evolution of mind.

The environment of the mind is our cultural environment, our source of learning. Cultures change rapidly with the flood of new information. As rapid as information change is, our very complex brain seems to still take many years to adapt. We see this clearly in the history of science, with one discovery after another. The human brain treats its existing ideas as its identity and protects those ideas with survival behavior. This process makes change generational. We see the future with the lens of our past experience. We excuse this generational phenomenon by accepting that new information is not accessible or applicable until the culture is ready for it. That is, until it is massively undeniable. It is interesting that the evolution of mind carries with it the evolution of its relevant environment. The flood of information invokes a flood of new technology to support adaptation, an environmental change not available in genetic evolution.

Religion promises stasis in a rapidly changing culture. If change is pain, no change must imply no pain. Yet we now have a crisis in losing membership. We see clearly that we must adapt, but how can we adapt if we define ourselves as unchanging. Just what is it that is causing our loss of membership? Is it really inability to adapt? Is it that our market is disappearing? Are we losing our share to other institutions, other systems? If we are going to adapt, what is it that we can change that will not threaten our core beliefs?

What is it that could make our core beliefs recognizable as time and culture independent? We have a natural process called secondary process thinking designed to strengthen of our identity. In large part our identity is the sum of our stored learning. Secondary process thinking is a process of comparing our childhood learning to adult logic. What is illogical is eliminated. When we justify spiritual beliefs, we use the proposition of faith. A child cannot distinguish real from unreal. To a child, spiritual ideas are truths, confirmed by adults, particularly parents.

A child's identity is relatively fixed by the age of 5-6 years. Immersing a child in spiritual ideas in this period imprints them in that identity for life. If the parents treat spiritual ideas as optional, the child can become ambivalent, but may not lose the imprinting. Repetition is a learning process that involves many different mental processes. The mind does not distinguish between words and thought in creating memory. It records everything. You get to remember what you think and talk about most. Those memories become who you are.

Through mind we communicate with God. Our mind, through evolution, is God's creation. Our mind, like muscle, works on the "use it or lose it" principle. The brain utilizes as much as 20% of the body's energy. To conserve energy, the brain enters a process of eliminating about half of its neurons that are unused or little used. This process begins after age of 10 and lasts through the mid-20s. New neurons can be generated in relation to the degree of use of the mind in experiencing new events. Peak learning occurs in the first 10 years of life and is foundational. Yet, to protect the child's social development, we limit the formal learning process for half that period.

We humans are driven by the pleasure principle. This is the basis for our need to learn delayed gratification. We need to strike a balance between pain and pleasure, or at least, pleasure and no pleasure. Change is pain. Change requires work. We are in danger of taking the path of least resistance and slipping into a posture of recreation. Can we season the work of change with a jot of recreation? It is clear that nature demands balance in all things. We live in a diverse world, a world of dynamic opposites. We worship rugged individualism, a challenge to diversity. We are called not only to accept diversity, but to rise above it, to transcend self in building loving relationships.

The question is then, would our Religion be more robust if we read and teach the Bible in the context of how God's creation works? The *Bible* is taken as the validation of God, but there is no evidence or logic to prove God's existence. The Bible validates that man's emotional behavior has not changed noticeably from Biblical times to the present. Man's behavior seems timeless. It is the Bible's supernatural events that create doubt. The idea seems to be that supernatural events validate God's presence. Yet, God's creation is natural. In understanding God's creation, we see that supernatural events do not occur, or occur rarely, or with great subtlety. It is the cultural shift of over 2000-3000 years that has returned supernatural events to the imaginings of the story tellers. Does this demean the *Bible*? It depends on our expectations. Does our learning demand absolutes, I musts, I demands, or does our learning have room for both the logical and the metaphorical?

In all of this, we ask the question of whether God can exist in the modern world. Does God micromanage? Here we get into the way God's world works, and particularly the Mind. It has been nearly 14 billion years since the Big Bang, when our universe probably started. With evolution as God's creation tool, it took about 10 billion years for life to begin and another nearly 4 billion years for evolution of life to the level of Man. The evolution of the cerebrum, our logical brain, began 15 million years ago. With Mind, we became aware of God. That is, God had to wait nearly 14 billion years for Man's awareness of God. In that sense, for man, God came into existence with man's awareness, just a few years ago. Clearly God is not dead. He exists. He exists in the minds of his followers (half the world population). He is just not real. Here we have the best example of the confusion in naming. When we know God, we don't just believe in God. He is in our feelings. We feel his presence. Through our emotions God breaks into our behavior and becomes a physical force. His real/physical works are then on display in the world.

For a thousand years, the Church told everyone what to think about God under penalty of death. When biblical logic began to crack, many different denominations developed over the following period of so-called enlightenment. This was of course facilitated by the invention of the printing press. Thus began the idea of an educated public and of intellectual freedom. For the next five hundred years, attending church in one form or another was still a cultural requirement. Then a series of events followed that took control away from established religious leadership. It began with the weakening of the family and consequently the Church.

1. Women entered the work force.
2. Families became mobile and separated with the development of National and Global Business.
3. Economics and ideas about overpopulation led to a reduction in family size to a level that threatens to eliminate our culture.
4. Our culture has accepted competitive alternatives to religion such as TV sports and Sunday soccer.
5. Commitment to Church support has been weakened by the trend away from family operated business and toward professional management.
6. There has been a shift away from church endowment to endowment of foundations.
7. The loss of manufacturing has reduced the average income and shifted downward average Church gifting.
8. Much immigrant population is now non-Christian, and conversion is a generational task.
9. The idea of separation of church and state has been utilized by anti- religious groups to make any public expression of religion illegal or politically incorrect.
10. The weight of scientific discovery made biblical thought contentious.

As religion has become weakened, other activities have been given a competitive advantage. As children move into other states or nations to meet job requirements, the idea of a family church has weakened. Family businesses no longer are a mirror for employee preference for a church or denomination. With the standard of living trending downward and the wealthy shifting away from church endowment and toward funding through foundations, churches are left with expensive properties that they can ill afford to maintain. Healthy churches require double and triple their typical local church membership. Deficit spending consumes energies that should be directed toward missions. Dwindling budgets mean smaller and fewer missions.

Like it or not, the control expressed in early cultures led to strong identities. As cultures mature, they experience less threat and become less controlling. This leads to fuzzy boundaries and graying traditions. Controlling gives way to balance and ideas of balance give way to ideas of equality. For religion, all this change means the loss of fertile ground for growth. Instead of facing a new crop of indoctrinated young, we face ambivalence. To these, we are not bringing truth. The stories have lost meaning. We fall back on recreation to attract, but this is not who we are. It threatens our identity.

If we are to be fishers of men, then we must think seriously about what kind of bait we need. We have a particular story to tell that is timeless and universal. Is it not selling because the story is wrong? I think not. It is not selling because we don't know what kind of bait to use. The story is to love God and to love our neighbor. Why is this story culture and time independent? Science says that it reduces stress and increases life span. It is a healthy way to live. Psychologists and philosophers say that it is self- transcendent and can give life meaning. Macroeconomists say that it supports stability over equality. What these ideas leave out is the need for unconditional love. That is, unconditional acceptance. How do we deliver unconditional love utilizing a parish that by nature is a mixed bag of welcoming and unwelcoming behavior? Before we can deliver, we need to heal ourselves and make that healing, or at least that healing process, visible in the community. It would seem that it is not so much the product as the vehicle by which the product is sold that requires change.

Just as all of nature is diverse, we would expect that parishes differ in their identity and therefore in their group personality. We can't be all things to all people, so who are the people most likely to find confirmation in our particular product? We have a waning elderly whose early indoctrination is still aflame. We have an older group in which the artifact of childhood immersion is still smoldering. We have the children who are open because they are children and parents who are perhaps smoldering, or perhaps who buy the fact that a belief system is a requirement for good health, or perhaps for the promise of good behavior. We have adults who recognize they have the need for a social network and are not satisfied with sports, the bar scene, or work buddies. We have the lost and the indifferent. All these people have a common human element. They are a mixed bag of good and bad behavior. That is, good behavior that is life-enhancing and bad that is life-defeating, and each in different degree. What they all need is unconditional love, regardless of their behavior or circumstances, but we can't package that. We have to act it out. We have to make it our works, such that people can see and know who we are.

Chapter XXVII

Paradox

What we want most in life is what we are least likely to get. This is sometimes called a reverse script. It is because wanting something intensely makes us aggressive in our pursuit of it. This opens the door to illogical behavior that pushes away what we need most to fulfill our desire. The paradox: to gain life we must lose it. To gain control we must give up control. To create loving relationships, we must give up ourselves by listening to others. Loving relationships offer us the opportunity to be what we want to be, and with the people we want to be with. To get love, we must give love.

Paradox is like a joke. In a joke the teller leads the listener to an obvious place and then sets him or her down in an entirely different and unexpected place. In the Paradox, the participant through his or her expectations and perceptions follows the path to a particular place. The goal of the participant has its own separate character or identity. Upon arrival, the participant at the chosen place finds it the opposite of their expectation.

Many *Bible* stories that were understood as stories in the past have become truths for many people as a result of repeated telling and changing culture. The paradox in this case is a paradox in the context of belief and disbelief. To the believer Jesus as God is both truth and paradox. To the disbeliever it is simply untrue.

The brain has evolved to have the ability to take repeated information and create an idea that is perceived by the participant as real. This involves expectation. An unrealized expectation in some circumstances becomes a paradox. A marathon runner practices for several years to win the big race. He can visualize his success, but loses. The runner cannot believe the result but retains his vision, the expectation.

It is common enough to find people whose core beliefs involve a "must have", or an "I demand". Must and demand needs are the result of early trauma that shapes self-defeating learning. It results in unstable, toxic relationships that consume the participants with anxiety. The participants are not what they want to be and certainly are not with those they want to be with.

It is unfortunate that the characteristic behavior of a personality with a "Must" or "Demand" in his or her core belief is often perceived as strength of character and is deemed suitable for leadership. Such irrational behavior can easily reside beside very positive character traits, becoming evident only under pressure. Thus, we can have the paradox of a charismatic leader that is also a tyrant. It is when we experience an individual with both character traits in play that we feel an assault on our expectations.

A person's Illogical, self-defeating behavior is rooted in their subconscious mind. They experience an event, an emotional trigger, as an attack on the self. The response is automatic. Conflict—Anxiety—Anger. Anger creates an anger response. It's the way the primitive brain works. We hear of children shooting other children because someone has been disrespected. Road rage is another example. Understanding such addictive behavior is the "booby prize". Understanding is not a cure. People with illogical behaviors are unlikely to perceive the paradox: to gain control, they must give up control.

CHAPTER XXVIII

FREE WILL

Systems Theory brings up two issues, free will and determinism. The common meaning of free will is that God has given humanity a choice in how he or she will live his or her life. The net assumption is that God is responsible for the good in the world and man is responsible for the bad. The problem with this view is that it doesn't seem to match the way the world works. Each person as an individual is the sum of early learning and genetics. Both of these are diverse, diverse in environment, and in genetic makeup. Our mental system for learning records and processes whatever sensory input it receives. Bad infects good and good infects bad. In this view, where is the free will? Can we be proactive rather than reactive in responding to the negative events in our lives?

Determinists believe that the Universe is preordained by God. The net assumption is that humanity is on God's bus and must endure the ride. This leaves one with a sense of impotence. With no control, there is no sense of purpose. Even if God has a purpose, we have not been asked to participate in the process. We value what we work for. Some suggest that if we, as living systems, live by the rules of God's systems, then we have no control over our lives.

There are a variety of phrases like "thou shall not judge lest ye be judged". "People who live in glass houses should not throw stones." There is an underlying dynamic in this that man has some relationship problems that require constant attention. If the Bible is man's interpretation of his own journey through life, it is not surprising that someone has to be blamed for the bad. Christians might blame the devil for their poor choices, given free will. The determinists might blame God because he predetermined it all.

We might consider the idea that free will has nothing to do with being bad or good. Suppose that free will is simply permission to call God. The God that is with us, in our mind, in that inner world, is available to listen to each of us. It is our free will to call or not to call. Given the diversity of our behavior, reflected by an imperfect system, God acknowledges the limitations of his systems and humanity, and offers forgiveness as a remedy. We are free to take the medicine, or not to. That is also free will. Good and bad are artifacts of diversity and evolution, not the will of God.

It is surprising how many people interpret a rule system as a threat to freedom. Actually, most rule systems are designed to increase freedom. It is a matter of balance. You can see a red light as preventing you from exercising your choice to proceed. There is less emphasis on the fact that red lights prevent accidents. Accidents are more limiting. Nature's rule systems are preordained. Evolution creates a diversity of both positive and negative events. Our responses can be difficult, even painful, but they give us life. Change is pain, but change we must. Do such systems imply no control or participation? Systems survive and transcend by the process of individual agents joining together to motivate change. Transcendence is fuelled by the energy of individuals. Revolution is a bottom up process. Yes, we each have control. No, we don't have complete control. No, we can't do it by ourselves.

If I were to tell a story about free will, it would probably go like this: *The all-knowing God, imagining Creation, perceived that free will would be precious to humanity, his intended creation. God chose the best possible choice, evolution, as his creation tool so that man would receive this most precious gift. Thus, in God's time, man evolved to receive the most complex living system in creation, the human brain. God's choosing was not without risk. As a result of God's choice, this brain would collect and store whatever information it received. It would evolve identity, mirroring that information: good and bad, life-enhancing and life defeating. Thus, God gave man freedom and choice, and the ability to create, according to God's own image. Man evolved to the level to imagine God, but evolution is a continuum. Man, with free will, evolved further, creating alternatives to the yearnings for love and hope that were the intent of God. Man turned away from God.*

Without a God-intent, Man's imagining and creation became inward directed. There was no God purpose. There was no love of neighbor. There was only the self. This was devolution to a time before awareness of God, a time of fear and hopelessness, a time without meaning. This is a condition that, as before, evolves a yearning for God. As awareness of God dissolves, the yearning for God solidifies and the cycle of belief begins again. Man without God lives in a lonely, fearsome, and primitive place.

How many belief cycles are necessary to complete God's purpose? How do we break through this cyclical process? Will we recycle through eternity, or will we evolve enough to break out of our self-defeating survival behavior into a better future? We get to choose as projected in our behavior.

The cycle of belief is fuelled by the dynamic of opposites: fear vs. pleasure. The cyclical nature of belief requires fear for survival in primitive cultures. In modern cultures, there is time for pleasure and the funds to support it. Pleasure is the companion of wealth. We equate wealth to success. Yet, success breeds forgetting. Familiarity breeds contempt. The handmaid of wealth is responsibility, not pleasure. Pleasure is momentary. Ultimately, we all search for meaning to justify a life well spent. Life's meaning comes from loving relationships, not wealth, not power. Wealth without loving relationships is the worst kind of poverty.

Survival behavior that sustains wealth and power weakens with disuse. This provides the opportunity for a culture of predominantly loving relationships. We are left to imagine a cyclical rise and fall of culture from survival behavior to loving relationships. This cyclical process is typical of all of Nature's dynamic opposites that fill the evolutionary landscape: good vs. bad; strong vs. weak; rich vs. poor; obese vs. thin; tall vs. short; belief vs. disbelief. All of these attributes are fed into our personality development and into our resulting behavior. All of these color our expectations and perceptions, and thus our choices. Without a strong identity and belief system, we become reactive rather than proactive in dealing with the events that can overwhelm us.

Cyclical systems require feedback to supply the information required for efficient adaption to events. Without such regulation to hold the system within normal limits the system will fail, typically through polarization that clogs its information channels. A person with bipolar condition cycles from manic to depressive, with little middle ground of normalcy. Anorexia is a similar condition in fasting and gorging. With survival behavior belief and disbelief can fall into passionate opposition. Belief brings with it a set of ideas for healthy living that support a normal balance between a life- defeating vs. a life enhancing life style. Disbelief, through free will, opposes belief, creating optional paths away from God and can be used in justifying the self-defeating life styles of those who resist rule systems.

Life is not an equal opportunity process. Loving relationships, life- enhancing life styles, spiritual growth, require us to give support to those less well off. While we are genetically the same, the diversity of events in our lives makes us uniquely different in our identity. We each view the world through that unique identity. This diversity is context in which we use free will to choose our path. With free will comes responsibility. We are challenged to do the best we can with the skills and abilities we have, and within the environment in which we are embedded. No part of God's Creation is without love. It is you that have the opportunity to find it, or create it.

CHAPTER XXIX

LOVE

C.S. Lewis talked and wrote about four types of love: Storge, Eros, Philia and Agape. Storge defines the love of parents for their children. This is best thought of as the unconditional love we instinctively have for small children. As children get older, we find ourselves in the dilemma of having to direct and discipline them, sometimes giving them "tough love". Love at the level of discipline is about regulation that is a life long challenge of setting limits. Setting limits challenges our instinctive need for freedom and choice. Balancing this act will have major impact in forming the expectations of a child and thus his identity. As we have said, this happens in the first 5-6 years. At this stage, love becomes more like Agape, Christian love. Agape is the commitment to the spiritual growth of one's self and others. Agape involves work. Scott Peck says that love is work and that the work of love is mainly listening. In listening, we validate the other person.

This process of moving from Storge to Agape is much like the process of moving from Eros to Agape. Eros is romantic love. This, like Storge is instinctive. Eros is emotional and hormonal, a feeling of euphoria that requires no work. It is a basic, animalistic emotion that is intended by nature to support population growth. As we have moved from an environment of low to high population, Eros has tended to move away from population support toward some mix of self and mutual gratification,

Erotic relationships can evolve over time toward Agape. The statistics, however, say that it is a 50-50 proposition. There is a saying that success breeds forgetting, and another, that familiarity breeds contempt. Erotic love gets wrapped up in the need for self-esteem. As this need lessens, the need for self-gratification lessens. There is then room for a more mature love that involves helping one's companion or spouse to grow toward enlightened self- esteem. This again is the work of love, more like Agape.

When we think of love as having four different definitions, we should also be thinking of love as a continuum. The four expressions of love have separate faces, but are also one face. The mind has many parts, systems within systems, and systems in relationship with other systems. While we pass through the various expressions of love, we are not in a replacement process. We are experiencing a change in utility of one over another. As we gain in wisdom, we experience an unconscious change in relative value, a preference that better fits our present being. Lasting love requires room for individual identities to thrive. The question becomes who am I that my identity fits a love for one's neighbor as one's self? If there's no fit, what then… change?

As human beings, we are constantly adding to our stored learning. This changes our perception of ourselves and changes our priorities, conscious or unconscious. Our mind "has many mansions". We have a sub-personality, or face, or part of our mind called "the Judge". The Judge is supported by our need for control. The Judge tends to label our mental parts as good or bad… "In with the good, Out with the bad." Those parts called bad tend to be locked up or caged and not allowed to express themselves. Often their existence is denied. The more we lock these sub-personalities away the harder they fight for expression. The result is an increasing drain on our energy to keep these unwanted parts hidden. They represent the mask of our self which we carry as a burden that can exhaust the radiance that is our real self.

The nature of evolution of Mind is the diversity of learning and resulting behavior as we are impacted by life's flow of mixed events. The majority of us fit in a population with a mix of some good and some bad characteristics for lasting love. Nature's intent is to hide these seeming small differences under an erotic drape. "Love is blind". As we mature, the drape falls away and we are challenged to deal with these seeming small differences that grow out of proportion. We are then required, through our individual identity, to deal with conflicting expectations. We either walk away or choose to adjust our expectations by acknowledging this natural diversity. We then must deal with just how much we can adjust without moving outside the boundaries of our unique identity. How much can the willow bend?

Narcissism is self-esteem at a level that limits or eliminates caring relationships. There is no love in narcissism because there is no spiritual growth. It is obsessive self-esteem. To talk of self-esteem as equivalent to self-love requires the qualifier, 'enlightened'.

CHAPTER XXX

THE WAY THE WORLD WORKS

The world has evolved over the past 14 billion years, first as energy into matter, and then as matter into non-living, then living systems. The first step took about 10 billion years, the second an additional 3.8 billion years. These transformative years were marked by natural laws, the physical and chemical processes by which evolution created its diversity and then with living systems adaptation for survival. Natural instability and decay of high molecular weight elements place an upper limit on the diversity of matter. Living systems, adapting to their changing environment, have evolved to a complexity to exhibit Mind, the human brain being the most complex living system in our world.

While we are well aware of the rules of physics and chemistry by which our world works, we have only recently become aware that there are rules by which living systems work. Whether a cell, tissue, an organ, a body, an individual, a family a community, a state, a government, all are separate, interdependent, living systems and all operate to system rules. All are aware of their particular environment. All adapt to that particular environment with a primary directive to survive. All have a particular mission or purpose. All are stabilized by webs of relationships with the systems in their primary environment. All have processes of ingestion, digestion, excretion, growth and reproduction. All are self-organizing and self-healing. All seek stability, homeostasis.

At some point in the evolution of Mind, human living systems became self- aware. With self-awareness came feelings of loneliness and awareness of the finiteness of life. Survival was not just a response to an incident, but a continuing fear of losing life. A lightning storm was not just an incident. It became memory and feelings of dread continued after the incident. What followed were attempts to deal with these feelings by developing relationships and creating ideas about unnatural sources of protection such as gods. With socialization, these processes and ideas became the basis for cultures and over time became truths.

Over time, a few thousand years, people moved from memory and story telling to reading and writing. It was just a matter of time before reading and writing moved from a specialization to common knowledge. This led from a diversity of thoughts and feelings unexpressed, to a diversity of thoughts and feelings projected in behavior and in the written word. This made possible our unquenchable quest for knowledge, moving from private collections of books, to public libraries, to search engines on the internet. In recent time, our science and technology has begun to broach the final frontier of Medicine, the human mind. We seemed poised to experience an age of enlightenment that mirrors that period in the 17th century.

We are now faced with a time continuum as expressed in the process of evolution. This continuum extends backward to the smallest known particles, bosons, and forward to the complex compounds supporting life and mind. Science has chosen to define their segment of this continuum as those things that are measurable. This extends from bosons to the physical brain, excluding consciousness and mind. This mind partitioning defines the province of psychology and religion as unreal, though behavioral therapy has its basis in the reality of behavior which is measurable and might be considered behavioral science. One might ask if behavior resulting from religious belief is an area for scientific study. Religion accepts all of creation, but struggles to accommodate the discoveries of science. Separation of the physical world from the world of mind has played a significant part in defining human culture.

CHAPTER XXXI

THE STRUGGLE FOR BALANCE

Have you ever wondered why we strive to 'end world hunger', to 'free the world of disease', to 'end all war'? We don't just want to keep them in a practical balance. We want them gone. There have been several grand attempts to create utopian societies and communes. They don't work. The world doesn't work that way. There are two problems, them and us. Actually, there is massive diversity in Nature, differentiation from one end to the other. There is a diversity of disease, of environment, of human sensitivity, of wealth, etc. etc. etc. Nature is diverse. It's the way the world works. Diversity is a natural consequence of evolution. Nature deals with diversity by providing feed-back systems and resistances to limit the range of unbalance. At the macro level those are selection, adaptation and time. Well meaning and hopeful visions of equality over diversity are unnatural. They are disruptive, chaotic, and lead to system failure.

Nature is made up of systems and systems within system... self-organizing, self-maintaining, self-healing... interdependent systems. Living systems: bacteria, people, corporations, governments, all follow systems rules. Each complex living system survives in relation to its own sub-systems and to its own environment of associated systems. As systems evolve, they diverge. Over evolutionary time many varieties appear due to mutation. Most disappear due to poor environmental adaption, and to major and minor extinction events.

As living systems adapt over time they become increasingly complex. As the fittest living systems survive and become increasingly complex there is thought to be a convergence supported by natural selection. Some think that human evolution may be associated with such a convergence, though there is no indication of an end point to our convergence in evolutionary time.

Man sits at the current top of the evolutionary pyramid, having reached a level of complexity that exhibits mind. The human brain is the most complex system in the universe, with as many dendrite connections as there are stars in the universe, some 40 quadrillion. The limbic system of man's brain has evolved over 450 million years, giving rise to man's survival nature. The cerebrum, particularly the frontal lobes and anterior cingulate, has evolved over the past 15 million years, giving rise to man's creative ability and compassion. Thus, we have a tenuous balance between the (old) limbic brain and the (new) cerebrum, the amygdala vs. the frontal lobes and anterior cingulate. The amygdala, the source of emotion, provides the 1000 pound elephant, anger that dominates over empathy and compassion. On an evolutionary scale, the new brain is still in diapers. We have a long way to go before humanity learns to live in loving relationship, a natural balance that is the way the world might someday work.

History is filled with stories of systems that were born, grew, matured, aged and became extinct. Many of these stories have a common theme of robust growth and then failure due to poor adaptation to changing environment. Death is about the lack or inefficient use of information, resulting from breakdown of the information pathways that carry the information needed for adapting. This is the story of evolution: adapt or die. It's the way the world works. The natural balance of complex living systems results in homeostasis. All living systems seek homeostasis.

As complex living systems at the top of current evolution, at least in complexity, we are aware of our environment and aware that we are aware. We protect our self, responding to our primary directive.

We are systems within a greater system and have responsibility for the survival of our self, our environment and our greater system. In the pursuit of self, we strain our relationships. History has given us the insight that the ultimate meaning of our lives is in the freedom and choice to transcend our sense of self and to become one with our environment and our greater system. This is also the way the world works. The common tendency is to exalt the self at the expense of our transcendent responsibility to others.

It becomes clear that complex living systems at our state of evolution require a feedback system (policing) and limits to variation from normal balance (regulation). As much as we are imbued with an instinctive need for freedom and choice, our behavior as a people tends toward self-defeating. The age old questions are whether and how can we evolve beyond our self-indulgent, self-defeating nature before we destroy our specie. What is new in the history of life on earth is humanity's development of means for self- extinction. It seems that we now must find a new directive to move beyond survival behavior to a new behavior of building caring relationships. This is the subject of religion. Science and technology without religion leaves us hanging by a very thin thread of caring relationships.

"Religion, the opiate of the masses", is a common phrase among the haves. The translation is that religion acts to preserve the natural balance between the haves and the have-nots. It seems that in this, the haves confirm the need for and a responsible party for a natural balance. This is best handled by the Government. The Government then must seek a distribution of wealth that is acceptable to the wealthy while avoiding revolution by the have-nots. Until the have-nots are driven to the point of revolution, the haves are in a position to pressure for the status quo. This process becomes delicate when the Government as a system begins to act in its own interest (Grow or die).

Lobbying, corporate payoffs, complexity of laws (irrelevant, hidden amendments), excessive size (too big to fail; too many jobs to lose), loss of a national language, poverty, immigration, unregulated capitalism; socialism, etc. are all tools for manipulation of the natural balance. These become devices to clog the information pathways and stifle relationships. The unbalance results in stress that causes polarization of parallel systems. Polarization facilitates system breakdown, leading to failure.

Religion provides institutions that pressure the system for natural balance. Yet, religions are under attack by the legal system (ACLU) and atheistic groups that are essentially haves. Traditional religions are losing membership. The size of membership is essential for leverage in any activity. The ship of Government is tipping over and the counterbalance systems of religion and positive change are turned off. If there is no place for religion in Government, is there justification for an active part for religion in the macroeconomics supporting Government? The systems view of how the world works seems a practical way to gain insights into the struggle for natural system balance. Operating counter to the way the world (Nature) works is a poor strategy.

CHAPTER XXXII

POWER LAW

A persistent complaint among people in any society is the inequity in the distribution of wealth... the rich get richer and the poor get poorer. It is easy to blame individual behaviors such as greed or indifference. Studies in the distribution of social networks indicate that these explanations are wrong, or at least, beside the point. What matters is that diversity plus freedom of choice create a natural inequity, and the greater the diversity, the more extreme the inequality. The phrase power law results from the fact that it describes a mathematical statement, a formula like P = (m/a)k that contains a value that has an exponent, a value raised to some power. This, when plotted, forms a shape we think of as a hockey stick laid down with the foot sticking up. The tight curve of the hockey stick we call a knee. Once the knee is formed, the shape rises rapidly. Income grows this way as do the spread of diseases, cancers, and population.

In systems where many people are free to choose between many options, a small subset of the whole will get a disproportionate amount of income (or whatever) even if no members of the system actively work towards such an outcome. This has nothing to do with moral weakness or any psychological explanation. The very act of choosing, spread widely enough, and freely enough, creates a power law distribution.

Power law distributions have spawned a number of catchphrases like the 80/20 rule and the Winner-Take-All Society. We are so used to the bell curve distribution (fat in the middle and skinny at the ends) that power law distributions can seem odd. Power law distributions arise in social systems where many people express their preferences among many options. As the number of options rise, the curve becomes more extreme. This is counter- intuitive: most of us would expect a rise in the number of choices to flatten the curve, but in fact, increasing the size of the system (more choices) increases the gap between the beginning number and the middle number.

A second counter-intuitive aspect of power law is that most elements or agents in a power law system are below average, because the curve is so heavily weighted toward the top performers. Adding the very wealthy produces a plot or curve that is called the 'L' plot. As a system develops, new entrants are more likely to be influenced by earlier entrants. What matters is that any tendency towards agreement in diverse and free systems, however small and for whatever reason, can create power law distributions.

We live in a society driven by "The American Dream". Success is wealth. Income is a power law system. Is there inequity? Yes. Is it fair? Perhaps it is. If the majority of the people believe in wealth as an expression of success, then they must support the inequity. Are there potential new entrants that have equal or more skills than the wealthy? Yes. Will they therefore be successful? Most likely they will not. The distribution of new entrants follows the same power law. The number of the most successful will be proportionally lower. The system will get more robust, but the plot shape will remain the same. We seem faced with the fact that to change the inequities, we would have to reduce freedom and choice.

An interesting discussion that has been going on for years is the movement of manufacturing jobs to countries that have a low wage scale. Once this starts, all competing companies are forced to follow to maintain competitive pricing. This initially has the benefit of providing low cost products that particularly benefits the have-nots. As manufacturing increases the wage scale of the foreign source, companies are forced to move to the next competitive supplier. This power law process leads to more and more complex parts supply and finally to complete product line supply. This is followed by national brands. The originating companies in the final stages lose all manufacturing and become marketing companies.

We kid ourselves by saying that we will be the technology producer. More than half the seats in our technology colleges and universities are filled by foreign students. The growth in manufacturing in foreign countries provides the funding for educating vastly more scientists and engineers than we turn out. We no longer have the manufacturing jobs to support the education of our students. Our suppliers have become our competitors, using our educational powers and our technology.

We might think that this typifies the evolution of all industry. Our foreign suppliers are often not subject to power law. Their forms of government have rigid control of freedom and choice. Power law does not function under totalitarian governments whose regulations are absolute. It is clear that companies whose priority is the welfare of its employees and way of life would not seek profit at their expense. The unregulated exponential growth that is typical of all systems requires a cyclical reversal to survive. Exponential growth outruns its supply. The pursuit of wealth for its own sake is toxic. At the conclusion of each of these thought processes, we ask, "where are the ideas of intrinsic rightness and religious principles which seek moderation and balance?" They are being suppressed. Who then is going to regulate the regulators?

Is there a practical way to reduce the power law impact while maintaining an acceptable system operation? That is, can we disrupt power law; change the rules? Yes, by eliminating freedom and choice. Again, it's about balance. In the big picture, flexibility within the system is essential to avoid system extinction. As Christians, we might perceive that changing our concept of success by adding a large dollop of empathy and Christian charity would be helpful. Flexibility is defined by the power elite. We have many historical governments that have fallen to inflexibility. Systems theory suggests that when the webs of relationships (information pathways) become rigid and clogged, indecision and sluggish response destroy the system. Looked at another way, it is the natural tendency for systems to protect previous learning over new learning. This clogs the information pathways. "You can't teach an old dog new tricks".

Chapter XXXIII

Is Systems Theory Anti-God?

The consensus of scientists over the past 80 years or so is that Systems Theory, though not a classic theory, is worthy of scientific theory status. This is because it so closely matches observations of the scientific community that it justifies that status. This conclusion is not unlike that of the Theory of Evolution. We can then assume that our world is made up of living and non- living systems all of which follow system rules. Systems Theory is a broad view of how the world works.

We cannot understand the context of anti-God without understanding the context of God. Our proposition of faith is that there are truths that cannot be proven by evidence or logic. On this basis, we make the assumption that God exists. We don't know that God exists in the same way that we know an automobile exists, through physical experience. We say that we believe he exists. Yet coming to believe is a learning process. What are the events that support this God belief process? There are no facts, no evidence. We can know that we have an idea of God, but we have no measurable fact of God. Jesus said, "See him in my works to know and believe that he is in me and I in him."

We come to believe and know through physical experiences. We can observe a multitude of physical results of the behavior of God believers, from Sunday meetings to cathedrals, from music to paintings to statuary. These are symbols of God, but are not God. We have the teachings of Jesus as the best way and a healthy way to live. All these are ideas or the physical expression of ideas. We have a yearning for God that inclines us toward belief. Ultimately, we are forced back to our proposition of faith. In matters of faith, we consciously or unconsciously choose to believe.

Since we come to believe and know through our physical experiences, an interesting question is whether we can choose to believe, or whether, as the catastrophe definition of Catastrophe Theory suggests, the weight of accumulation of one type of experience over another at some level precipitates catastrophe, sudden change. Do we choose to believe consciously, or do we unconsciously cross an invisible boundary of change? I say that I have chosen to believe, but I am not aware of the number and degree of experiences that may have accumulated in my mind to make this choice for me.

It would seem that we cannot know that God exists through physical experience. Yet, we believe that he exists. What is this about? We have been given a creative mind. We have also talked some about how the mind as a memory system can create new ideas in relation to previously stored ideas, gaining in creative potential through layer upon layer of ideas. The rudimentary learning of language, numbers and relationship are the earliest form learning and the tool box for greater learning and idea generation. On this basis, our early ideas about religion and God form the basis for the mind's process of generating higher levels of ideas and awareness of religion and God. To the extent that we think about and talk about, and spend our time in a religious environment, we will create whatever believing and knowing these experiences, physical or mental, that we consciously or unconsciously choose.

To some all of this might seem heretical. It utilizes the way creation works to try to understand God and our relationship with God… perhaps, the God of Mind. Religious thought and God have their residence in Mind, in our inner world. What we physically experience is the result of humanity's belief in God. Complex living systems and Mind are the creation of God. We know from observation that physical systems exist. If we believe in God as Creator, then we believe that he created systems and the rules associated with systems. As Christians we are instinctive in our support for the idea of free will and the freedom to choose.

If God created the world, his creation tool for complex living systems was and is evolution. Evolution creates a diversity of options. Some options survive better than others. Environments undergo catastrophic change. Some species survive and adapt, others do not. Existence is no predictor of survival. As individuals we have an average life time. Perpetuity is about procreation. Epic environmental change can even eliminate this. We are given the opportunity to exist and to adapt, but with no guarantee.

The choice in whether and how to adapt is given to us. We are even given the choice to change our environment. Our ability to change our environment faster than we can maintain control of it is a challenge based on this choice. We are given the choice of how to adapt for survival. We are then subject to the possibility of a random extinction event, within the time span of our existence. Until that event, we are very much in control of our existence.

If we believe in God, we most likely believe that God has a purpose for humanity. We have evolved to the level to exhibit Mind. We have the most complex living system in the universe, the human brain. Was this the unexpected consequence of a complex system that is prone to unintended consequences? Was it God's intent to utilize evolution to create complex living systems so that humanity might develop? It appears that in the process of evolution there is a tendency for convergence. Can we choose to believe that we are part of a convergence toward some God purpose? To give our existence meaning, we need to believe so. The hope for something better is a mental construct that has the potential to set us free from the killing aloneness of self. We are created as social beings who seek relationship for survival.

We are complex living systems. To think that systems are anti-God seems an oxymoron. Does God create systems to fail or to oppose him? I choose to think not. I choose to think that God has utilized for his purpose the best systems and processes, i.e. evolution. All operate according to system rules. His choice does not guarantee it to be optimal in our experience of it. Bad things happen. It is the price of existence. I find it interesting that on the one hand we acknowledge that God is unknowable, and on the other, we are constantly trying to define him and his intent using our human references.

CHAPTER XXXIV

IS EVOLUTION ANTI-GOD?

I constantly think about diversity as an artifact of evolution, and yet, more than that. I think of evolution as a process, creating the ever-changing substance of physical being. The creation of knowledge requires a diversity of ideas, of non-substance. It would seem that any process which creates increasing complexity is evolving, is evolutionary, whether with or without substance, whether an appendage or an idea.

Evolution implies growth. Growth implies complexity. Environment supports evolution. Growth strains environment. Complexity is limited by the available requirements for its existence. It becomes clear that Nature abhors exponential growth. Complex living systems require restraint. Human systems, individual and group, have a long history of periodic unsustainable growth, initiating periods of reverse evolution, at the family level, the community level, the state level, the national level, and now the global level. Still, the need for growth is so strong that any form of restraint seems beyond reason. Any complex living system that becomes over-complex must revert to a lesser level of complexity or become extinct.

In spite of the reality of evolution as a scientific theory, the sad history of evolution as anti-God makes for a constant struggle to defend the overwhelming scientific evidence for evolution. The problem is that evolution's insights do not fit Biblical teaching for those who are literalists and those who are unaware of the science. For those of us who are aware of both the science and the Bible, for belief in God, we must find an acceptable middle ground, a balance.

I believe in God because I have an emotional need to do so. To me, evolution is obvious and evokes only curiosity. It is interesting that many believe that God created the universe, but are confused by the instances where evolution seems to be counter to a God purpose. I think that they confuse their man-like thinking with God-like thinking. If God created the universe, he created all the systems and processes in the universe. When we see systems and processes that obviously are counter to any logical God purpose, we decide that God didn't do it, man did, or Satan did. God did do it, but not intentionally.

We have many instances of evolution working backward. When we think about the creation of the elements in the periodic chart, we see that when evolution goes too far in assembling its atoms, the elements become unstable, and over considerable time, give off enough energy to return to a stable lesser element. What in the world happened with the dinosaurs? They were so successful that it took an epic environmental catastrophe to remove most of them, thus allowing lesser creatures, including mammals, an opportunity to evolve. This reminds us that chance is also involved. Nothing is guaranteed. The single celled animals which were the first step in creating complex living systems are also the most successful life on earth. Their simplicity fits almost any environment. They live in our intestines to help us digest food. Yet, these are also the successful killers of complex systems, including man.

Is it possible that we think too much about God as magical? Perhaps it is better to think of God as all knowing. Perhaps God used what was the best available for his purpose and that included universal cosmic laws, some of which we call chemistry and physics. Some of the events in the creation story are negative. I think that God is the God of purpose, not of perfection. He uses what is the best possible for his purpose. That we humans find some of the events in this process painful, or even lethal, is the sacrifice that both we and

God accept in support of a God purpose. As a benevolent god, God suffers our disease and our illogical, self-defeating behavior, as we do.

I cringe when some pastor, in his eulogy, says or implies that God has a plan for this or that child. For life to happen, death must happen. For good to happen, bad happens. Diversity with its dynamic of opposites is the way our world works. We have been given an incredible opportunity to exist. We are given the freedom to choose how to use it. This is not an equal opportunity process. God knows this. I believe that God created a self-organizing, self-sustaining, self-healing world. God does not micromanage. We have consciousness. We are each given Mind to create our own experience of God, or not to.

If we believe that God created the universe with evolution as his creation tool, then there are no gaps in the evolutionary process. There are just things that we don't or can't understand. We are not God. Lack of particular awareness doesn't mean non-existent, or error. The world, and evolution, works just the way God expects that it should. We and he both know that it could all reset itself with a chance extinction event. Our opportunity while we are here is to be part of a God-purpose that gives meaning to our lives. It is our choice.

Chapter XXXV

Religion is Small Potatoes

A newborn baby has no self. In this sense it is one with the universe, a state that requires years of meditation for adults to attain. The baby loses this wisdom as it gains its separate identity. It soon finds that he or she does not control the world. By the age of 5 or 6, the child has a relatively complete identity. By the age of about 12, the brain has changed to allow abstract thought. The age of fastest learning extends to age 10, then slowly declines, based on level of usage. It is said that a child exposed to a religion to the age of 7, is imprinted for life. Where in all of this learning does spiritual awareness come about? Is it intentional, or unintentional? It is said that a cradle atheist has no sense of God. Given a blank piece of paper, and asked to draw a sketch of god, they leave it blank. There is no imagining without a god experience. This suggests that the idea of God is learned. Given this learning, ideas about God are as diverse as the identities of individuals who think about God.

The fact is that at least 3.5 billion people think about God. Most of earth's population believes in some kind of spiritual, creative force. In response to this, we have a miniscule group of atheists instigating laws to restrict religious freedom to one's private residence, preferably out of public view. Church vs. State has become public vs. private. The blocking of public display of church behavior will destroy the church. The bedrock of religion is the process of building loving relationships. It is clearly meant to include other than family. Its intent is to provide a process for transcending one's own self-interests in support of others. This teaching is fundamental in our culture.

If religious practice is instinctive and most of the world practices some form of it, eliminating religious belief would then seem a form of mind control. Such a movement is clearly an attack on our civil liberties; certainly it is not in support of them. If religious institutions embody pressure for balanced government, in whose interest would a destabilized government be beneficial? It would presumably be the move toward a welfare state and big government, perhaps socialism. This accomplishment would require an instability that would shift power from the right to the left. This condition is supported by the polarizing of our two-party system. This has been accomplished. Destabilizing the Federal budget is a complementary strategy. This has been accomplished. Allowing the banks to buy the Congress has been a successfully implemented; Congress admits this. Where do we go from here??? Religion seems like small potatoes.

Wall Street, the new Government royalty, and the wealthy are the haves and the rest of us are the have-nots. This polarized atmosphere would have capitalism as the cause of all our problems. Capitalism is not perfect, but it has proven to be the consistent way to create wealth. How this wealth is distributed is the province of our Government. It writes regulations to control the processes of economic activity and levies income taxes to insure a stable distribution. Instability in the distribution of wealth occurs when individuals and groups find means to interfere with stable distribution.

The size of government, the complexity of its regulations and lack of some essential regulations act to support such manipulation; having no regulation is a death wish. Since it is the nature of our current population to be seeded with illogical, self-defeating behavior, it is unconscionable to suggest that we eliminate essential regulations again. Capitalism is a process for creating wealth. Like a gun or a stick of dynamite, it can be used for good or bad, depending on those controlling it. Most of the world's problems are not about processes and things. They are about self-defeating survival behavior.

The fact that the diversity of nature creates brilliant people who are equally profound in their greed seems to befuddle our systems of regulation which increasingly pander to such people in spite of periodic and traumatic reminders which occur about every five years. These familiar incidents are valid justifications for distrust of a government willing to subject a major population of its people to job loss, bankruptcies and foreclosures.

From a systems point of view, our Government is broken. Congress has lost the relationships required for communication, and with it, the ability to negotiate. This polarization and its results are well recognized. It must repair itself or our system will collapse into anarchy. A period of dictatorship is required to regain control. The steps to avoid such a collapse are well known and obvious. The question is whether the system will allow change to itself to prevent collapse. We are faced with the fact that large corporations and the very wealthy have bought the Government. The dynamic is deregulation vs. big government. We have Republicans and Democrats. Where are our Americans? Where are our institutions to pressure for balance? If we do not return to a stable, homeostatic state, our country will follow the historic path of government. This is the radical path, an illusion promising stress reduction. It is a coping method, leading to revolution and then a series of dictatorial governments over decades and perhaps centuries until a stable democratic form is reestablished.

We have said that systems large enough, with freedom enough and many choices, will follow power law. This is a mathematical relationship that indicates that the rich will get richer and the poor get poorer. It is a natural process. The only way to disrupt the excesses of this process is some level of regulation. Nature abhors unrestrained growth. It outruns its ability to adapt to change. It consumes the resources require for its survival. What institutions advocate moderation... the religious?

Perhaps the key advantage of inefficiency is increased time to adapt. Unfortunately, if at all, it is usually after the hole has gotten painfully deeper. The religious, the church, offer hope that the system will correct itself. That is equivalent to the hope for means to create a major and affective disturbance. I often wonder which is worse, big government, free markets, or theocracy. They all suffer from attracting illogical self-defeating behavior that is the human condition at this stage of our evolution.

CHAPTER XXXVI

Religion and Spirituality

The surveys show a trend of young adults moving from religiosity to spirituality. They also show a pervasive reduction in church membership. There seems to be some agreement that it is acceptable to be un-churched. Religion relates to a faith tradition that leads toward a god-head. Spirituality overlaps with much of religious tradition, but does not necessarily require belief in a god-head. If we take away the idea of a God, we take away the possibility of a god-purpose. We also take away the fire and brimstone imagery. Spirituality becomes a search for one's true self. We are left with the idea that humanity, in sum, has a purpose other than survival, or, as beautifully complex that Nature is, its self-organizing progress through time, however convergent its result, is purposeless.

Imagine time as a flowing river. Living systems enter the river at some time and space and travel downstream for a while. They then leave the river disassociating into nothingness. New systems assume their place. It is a closed system. The time of participating agents of the system gets used up like a fossil fuel. If the search for self is the total experience, there is no transcendence and no building of caring relationships. On the other hand, if the search for self includes a search for connection with the created world, it is could be the path toward God. The varieties and associations between religion and spirituality exemplify nature's diversity.

The human mind is the most complex living system in our universe. At some point in its evolution, Mind evolved the ability to create an inner world of thought and to imagine God. Spirituality would then suggest that God is a mental construct conceived in the human mind, probably as a survival mechanism, and that an alternative idea might be equally preferable. Most, perhaps all, of our basic mental processes are associated with fear, anxiety and survival behavior. Since there is this measurable shift in interest toward spirituality and self, and away from traditional religion, we can assume that it is fulfilling some definable need that traditional religion does not have the ability, or opportunity, to fulfill.

When we think about what we have learned about the brain and Mind, we realize that the nature of the learning system builds memory based on experiences. Based on this learning, we are able to create or imagine thoughts. Because we store both self-defeating and self-enhancing experiences, we can, in our inner world, create heaven, or hell, or some mix of both. Natural processes favor diversity.

Since we have a mixed bag of positive and negative behaviors, we have the option of minimizing our negative behavior and expressing a preponderance of positive behavior. While the choice seems obvious, negative behavior, survival behavior, is an expression of fear and anger, and anger is our strongest emotion and can dominate compassion. Hurt and humiliation cause our strongest memory imprints. When we seek to express life-enhancing behavior as the dominant expression of our being, we face a long, arduous challenge. As a result of natural diversity, some of us face a shorter path than others. Life is not an equal opportunity process. Fortunately, we now accept that meditation and self-talk, along with a positive environment make such change increasingly available.

Having said all this, we see that we have the option to create our personal world as one including God, or one without God. It is our choice. It's the way the Mind works. Actually, the way the Mind works is that belief and knowing are the result of the immersion of one's self in the subject of one's intention. That requires significant, repetition, time and focus on one's intent, whether that intent is religious or simply humanistic.

The stories, traditions and ritual of religion have been used to bring members into some form of "right behavior". Bartering for acceptance into the next life is strategy that doesn't fit adult logic. Nonetheless, it has been an essential part of the development of religious learning. The human brain does not develop the ability to deal with abstract though, such as the nature of God until about the age of 12, and past learning is valued over new learning. Adults carry with them their child learning experience long into adult life. This can lead to conflict as their expectations do not fit with adult experience. This weakens religion. One result is that atheists have dragged religion into the political arena, making it politically incorrect to talk publically about religion. Along with elimination of public expression of religious symbols, other pathways for immersion in religious thought are also eliminated. These are essential for religion's survival.

There is a large population that has suffered the abuse of religion at the hands of incompetent church leaders. The biblical logic teaches that religious learning is the only salvation process, opening the door for all sorts of control oriented behavior. A large part of psychotherapy is supported by individuals who have been forced to confront natural feelings with dogma and ritual that breed confusion and diminish self-respect. Diversity in self-esteem ensures that some people will respond negatively to what the majority experience as non-threatening. This is a mine field for church leaders. It often seems easier to leave a religion than to resolve a problem. Our legal system is committed to making this an acceptable path. Problems get solved by facing them, not by running away from them.

A question for religions is, "Why a preference for spirituality… because it is anti-religious? Is it lack of religious choice? Is it lack of religious freedom (inflexibility)? Is it lack of freedom (excessive control)? Is it the result of bad experiences? Is it boredom? Is it poorly defined benefits? Certainly, it is lack of immersion. That is, lack of religion as a quality image in membership minds. They don't own it.

They don't believe it. Belief in God is no different from becoming an accomplished musician. Both are an immersion process. You can't get there without it. It takes more than a weekly visit.

Atheism is anti-religious. Is it anti-spiritual? If we think of atheism in terms of the ample negative religious history, or the church vs. state issue, we realize that it is about fear of strong belief. Your choice is activism or non- activism. No effort is required. You join the parade. Christianity and spirituality take work at the individual level. You must do the work of building support for your decision to believe. This is an immersion process.

The science suggests that healthy minds take responsibility for their choices. *The New Testament* says that we can just believe and Jesus will take responsibility for us. This seems a much more compassionate message, given the diversity in our skills, abilities and the accessibility of that opportunity. Forgiveness does not imply the elimination of the self-defeating behaviors that we all have. I would assume that in the language of religion these negative behaviors are the cardinal sins that we are supposed to struggle against throughout life. The struggle is undeniable. In many ways, they separate us from God. A variety of psychotherapies are offered for behavioral problems. Relatively few people are brave enough to enter therapy. This leaves churches in a quandary. All are invited, but the environment created suffers. It seems we are sitting at the edge of chaos again, making tough choices, searching for balance, trying to love the barely loveable.

CHAPTER XXXVII

Philosophy vs. Religion

Philosophy is the investigation of nature based on logical reasoning rather than empirical methods. Philosophy includes the disciplines of science and the liberal arts, except medicine, law and theology.

Religion is the belief in and reverence for a supernatural power or powers regarded as creator, and the individuals and groups supporting such belief through their worship. Since philosophy does not include empirical methods, religion is not included in philosophy.

From the time of the establishment of the formal Catholic Church, the Church applied severe pressure to impose their religion on all humanity, with lethal penalties for thinking outside their biblical interpretation of nature. Since much of this dogma was patently false, church control over reason began to crack, leading to the "Age of Enlightenment". Galileo said that anything that could not be measured such as values and quality could not be a part of science. Descartes added that because religion was not measurable, it could not be included in science.

In modern time, we are apt to think of ethics and morals as the province of religion. On the other hand, many realize that they do not have to become churched to have an ethical and moral outlook.

Philosophy provides the same moral and ethical disciplines. It is the belief and reverence for a supernatural power or powers governing the universe that distinguishes most religions. What binds religions together is their intent and belief in a convergence toward a greater benefit for mankind. We call this the purpose of God for mankind.

The words "faith" and "belief" are often used interchangeably. Belief entails learning, where faith can be perceived as instinctive, or a potential for learning. We might think of faith as genetic. Perhaps genetics provide some people with the talent for a particular learning. For some, perhaps it is a path of least resistance.

We are constantly meeting new challenges to our traditional beliefs. We are coming to understand that people vary in their potential for ethical and moral judgments as a result of their biochemical processing. Hormonal imbalance can result in criminal behaviors. This challenges our religious notions of good and evil. We are in conflict on the subject of capital punishment. If the overriding purpose of our existence is to tilt the scale of good and bad toward the good side, is it ethical to let bad people survive to lead the good astray? The Bible says that the bad that occurs naturally in the world is forgivable, but woe be to those people who lead God's little ones astray; forgivable vs. unforgivable sin. Are "kill" and "murder" morally equal?

Are the religious dictates of 2000 years ago, in a very underpopulated world, directly applicable in today's over-populated world? Is it essential for each man and woman to face a death full of pain to purify their souls? Are pain killers immoral? Must we face a debilitating disease as our ticket to pass into paradise? The conflict caused by this cognitive dissonance tends to reduce faith and challenges belief.

While there is no proof that a universal creator god exists, the conception of such a god has persisted through the centuries in most cultures and is the basis for most religions. It seems evident that early gods were conceived to cover the range of positive and negative natural phenomena. Monotheism was a later concept. Associated with this development was the idea of a preserver and a destroyer mirroring man's positive and negative behavior. We see this in the

Hindu religion as Brahma, Vishnu and Shiva and in Christianity with God, Jesus and Lucifer.

Our traditional religions have their roots in antiquity. They bring visions of God and traditions that are thousands of years old. They are the result of a story culture, filled with symbolism, raising them to a level which forbids questioning. They are to be believed, not analyzed. Symbolism has become truth. We are caught in a highly educated world with primitive traditions resulting in the loss of their precious message.

Galileo and Descartes set the stage for the separation of science and religion. The advancement of science initiated the break away of the church's reliance on biblical scripture to define nature. That practice is still with us as creationism and the inerrancy of the Bible with notions of sentient life and soul at the cellular level (stem cell research). The Cartesian paradigm that life can be seen as mechanisms that can be disassembled and reassembled to obtain complete understanding, is giving way to a holistic paradigm that things are more than the sum of their parts, and that it is the dynamic relationships between the parts that support their stability. The development of Systems Theory and the brain scanning technology of MRI are beginning to make connections between the real and the unreal. Perhaps these developments indicate some convergence of science and religion.

This understanding of the relationship between parts or things has given rise to what has been referred to as Comparative Science. This is based on the insight that things that are obvious to scientists and yet not necessarily measurable can be defined as science. Comparative Science includes theories that are more like views or ways of thinking. Examples are Evolution, General Systems Theory, Complexity Theory, Catastrophe Theory, etc. This Comparative Science may be the bridge between science and religion. How this might play out is a question for Systems Theory. Will traditional religions be replaced by new religions with a language fitting our information age in the 21st century? Will traditional religions find the insights and language to adapt to the 21st century culture… perhaps some of both?

Chapter XXXVIII

Transcendence

All living creatures adapt to their changing environment or become extinct. This evolving process is coupled with genetic change in the creatures themselves. Both processes operate over great expanses of time. Living creatures have been evolving for close to four billion years. This time scale fits the gradual rate of genetic change. On the other hand, there have been sudden epic changes in environment that disrupted genetic mutation. In these short periods of time, species that could not meet the required rate of change are wiped out. It is not change which threatens complex living systems; it is the rate of change. With sudden environmental change, it is the larger animals that are most likely to succumb because of the lack of food and water. It was the elimination of most of the dinosaurs which allowed rodent size mammals to begin their evolutionary expansion. Finally, about 1.7 million years ago early humans, hominids, began to show in the fossil record.

Following the DNA chain back to its beginning, the human brain has been evolving for the past 450 million years. Fifteen million years ago the cerebrum (the logical, compassionate brain) began its evolution. This history of primitive, limbic brain vs. cerebral logical brain has set up a dynamic of opposites representing a typical natural pattern. Through its longer evolution, the wiring of the limbic brain with its fight/flight mechanism has been an essential mechanism for survival. All sensory nerve pathways go directly to the cerebellum in the limbic brain and were functional long before the evolution of the cerebrum began. The cerebrum is the seat of logic and compassion. The limbic brain is the seat of emotion, anger, survival response. As the various social processes make it less likely that the events we face are life threatening, cerebral function is given emphasis. Since anger is naturally a much stronger emotion than compassion, and since the limbic brain is wired for survival, survival behavior is typically dominant. Our logical, compassionate nature is secondary from an evolutionary perspective.

Our modern world is a very recent development, evolving exponentially over the past few hundred years. The modern world represents only about 14 percent of our world population. Eighty-six percent of our population is living in cultures where threat to individual safety is a common occurrence. Thus the culture of humanity is such that the vast majority live with an infrastructure and governance that makes survival behavior an essential part of daily life. This suggests that physical evolution of the cerebrum to support a culture of loving relationships is a long way off. If we imagine evolution of the mind, we might expect that the brain has already reached a level to support a positive expectation.

In the third world and in the ghettos of the first world, daily life is such that survival behavior continues as a primary component of personality. Children often have little opportunity to build the self-esteem essential to foster a strong, positive identity. The events of their lives often contain abuse and manipulation. The pressures of the modern world can have a similar impact on a child whose parents, during the child's critical growth years, are drawn into activities that leave the child without adequate nurturing. All these conditions lead to low self-esteem and resultant survival behavior. Without a healthy self-love, there can be little capacity to love others.

These intrusions of survival behavior have a negative impact on our ability to build caring relationships. As complex living systems, we seek meaning through relationships. Positive relationships increase self-esteem. A living system is a whole, whose stability results from webs of relationships. Relationships are information pathways that allow us to efficiently adapt to our environment. Because our learning system registers all of life's events, good and bad, we receive and store both good and bad information that we project in our behavior. Survival behavior, illogical, self-defeating behavior, based on that stored information, remains a significant part of our culture. We might wish it gone, but some level this aggressive behavior is an essential ingredient for success in any significant endeavor. Success is often associated with control psychology, the right and obligation to control others. Again, this brings us to the issue of balance, a natural balance in all things.

How do we limit self-defeating behavior? There are three requirements. 1) Immerse yourself in self-enhancing words, thoughts, information, 2) Control your tendency to respond negatively to your neighbor's self-defeating behavior, 3) find an environment supportive of self-enhancing behavior (your church). We might think of minimizing self-defeating behavior the same way we think about pruning a tree to improve its health. It is not a life threatening process. Emotions are feelings. We are not angry; we feel angry. Your brain, like muscle, operates on two principles: 'no pain, no gain' and 'use and disuse'. The more you use neurons, the more efficient they become. Likewise, unused stored learning tends to fade away as the brain discards little used and unused neurons.

The physical acts of behavior begin in the mind. You are known by your actions. Therefore, you are known by your stored learning. Your stored learning is who you are. The effort to change requires immersion in the new way of being. Change requires repetition… repetition… repetition. Change is work. Change is pain.

The process of change requires us to think about our stored learning in a different way. What we want to be is a person of enlightened self-esteem who projects his or her stored learning as self-enhancing behavior. This is the expression of your real self, living authentically. Your 3 pound brain, or 2.5% of body weight, utilizes 20% of the body's blood supply. Your brain is highly energy intensive. Self-defeating behavior is energy wasting. When you live authentically, you redirect that energy. You shine when you express your real self.

To express your real self, you do so through caring relationships. This is a personal process of sharing who you really are with others, encouraging a real response. This is the process of transcendence. You offer your authentic real self. This way of living is a process of taking the risk of sharing your real identity with others in the context of the spiritual growth of yourself and others. This is the way we are intended to be. In this we move emphasis from the evolution of the physical body to the evolution of Mind. Our ability to survive must be seen in this a new way of life. It is the epic environmental change in information that is presenting a rate of change that only Mind has the capacity to adapt to. The survival behavior of our pasts has limited application in a culture of loving relationships.

From the history of our global culture, it seems that the message of caring relationships is periodically rejuvenated by individuals and adopted by significant populations. It also appears that the message reaches some level of popularity and then fades as other ideas sap that energy. This is the typical cyclical pattern of opposing ideas. Our culture seems to mirror the evolution of our limbic and cerebral brain. Since under the best conditions our process of evolving must include the energy of survival behavior to motivate positive change, we cannot expect a perfect society.

As with all processes in Nature, we must look for balance and a level of moderation that allows time for adaptation to our changing environment. This would seem to fly in the face of our capitalistic society whose survival behavior seems to follow a cyclical process of emphasizing unrestrained growth, followed by the pain of broken dreams. This feast/famine cycle demands our culture to change drastically every 5 years, exhausting hope. Our new transcendent leaders will need to move the idea of caring relationships into the mainstream of life, but this cannot be done until it is realize that unrestrained growth is toxic and a self-defeating behavior.

Religious institutions should recognize the part they play in pressuring for moderation and balance. This is the message of creation. Whether individual or church, we follow the same system rules. We seek to transcend self, seeking a higher ground. We assume responsibility for the spiritual growth of our neighbor. As a church we are a greater system. Our neighbors are both individual members and greater systems. How is the church impacting its greater system neighbors: corporations, government, banks, Wall Street? How do we help them to grow spiritually (drag them to a higher ground)?

How do we preserve the best of the past while advocating living in the present and looking toward the future? We have allowed other systems to label us as politically incorrect. We have not yet accepted the challenge. My sense is that we must learn their language and challenge them on their own ground. We need to clarify our position as a higher ground. We need to challenge self-defeating behavior to send the message of hope for a better future. We need to regain the stature and relevance to reengage the populous with our transcendent message of hope and love.

CHAPTER XXXIX

A Better Way

Life and existence are generally acknowledged as real. It is what it is. That life is diverse is a given. The distribution of our population in the context of wealth is definitely, mathematically skewed toward the have-nots. Life as living systems, adapts to its environment. Then, at each place along the diverse distribution of existence there is a way of being that is a self- consistent and a normalizing dynamic. Each place has a stable existence in the context of that place and time. Again, living systems adapt to their environment. Sudden epic change in environment causes epic need for adaptation. Our new global fishbowl world has suddenly expanded the environment of about 70% of our world population, principally have-nots, giving new meaning to the word "poverty". We are again challenged to adapt. Scott Peck suggests that life is not about eliminating problems, but rather about learning how to handle more problems more efficiently. We desperately need a better way, but one that is realistic in the sense that it supports distribution of wealth in a way that does not collapse the systems that creates it.

Perhaps a better way of dealing with those things in life which seem to diminish our sense of being is not to eliminate them, but rather to change their context. Our expectations and perceptions of things in our life are a part of our stored learning. This suggests that rather than changing the issue, we might learn to perceive the issue in a different context. The old cliché is to see problems as opportunities. If the problem is overload, perhaps the Pareto Law applies. Focus on the 20 percent of activities that cause 80 percent of the problems.

Life overwhelms us with wants. If we differentiate between what we want and what we need and focus on need, we might get life back into manageable proportions, a return to scale. The ability to apply such thinking suffers its residence in only about one percent of the world population. There is perhaps only a few in any population who intuitively address context in their way of living. We are left with the obligation to be in caring relationship with the majority of the world population whose regional awareness has been assaulted by our global technology. We need to keep in mind that this population is the 86% that populate our world and whose survival behavior has the potential to overwhelm our arrogant minority.

All issues and events are in relation to our expectations and perceptions. Expectations and perceptions are mental constructs and are part of the inner world of Mind. We need to understand that this inner world was created by our mind, based on our thoughts about our existence, not about what our existence actually is or could be. Aware or unaware, we create our particular life through our choosing, but in the context of the particular events in our lives, in our particular environment. Our choosing is closely related to our expectations. When life gets unmanageable, stress is a symptom of the need to change.

We need to get to the realization that stored learning is the addictive way our mind creates memory. It is about repetition. In our inner world, we create for our self what we think about most. The same or similar information causes the dendrites on your neurons to move closer together with each repetition, making reception pathways stronger. In this way, your mind gives preference to what it has already stored. The more we think about the hole we think we are in, the deeper it gets. When we are in overload, what we think about most is overload.

Since we are the sum of our stored learning, we each, as a living system, protect that information as though our survival is challenged.

To change expectations and perceptions, we need to become aware that stored learning projects are who we are. To project who we need to be requires change in that stored learning, limiting self-defeating learning. This requires the flooding of our mind with positive, life-enhancing thoughts. What we think about most, we create as our inner world. What we do not use fades over time. Our mind seems to follow the 'use it or lose it' principle. Positive change is an immersion process.

The idea of turning negative thoughts into positive thoughts is a strategy to place an idea into a different context, rather than trying to eliminate it. We live in a diverse world. Both good and bad happen. We experience life-defeating events. We are not equally prepared to deal with such events. Negative stored learning from these events impacts some of us more than others. That is also nature's diversity.

There are, no doubt, other strategies to control rather than eliminate negative ideas. To make success real, it is essential to keep the idea of success in your conscious mind. Meditation and Self-talk are known processes for change. Accept the fact of your negative experience for what is, the past, an obsolete recording. It is not you. It survives only because you keep playing that record. Your brain utilizes 20% of your body's energy production. To save energy, our mind has evolved to minimize or eliminate the synapses and neurons that you don't use. An important way the world works is the freedom you are given to choose a better way of being. It is your choice to decide to live in the present and look toward the future. Acting on your freedom to choose requires a hopeful attitude, the commitment of time and energy to change, and a focus on life-enhancing ideas. Religion is a source of such ideas.

CHAPTER XL

SELLING PASSION

Who we are is our stored learning that results from the accumulation of life's events. Since our stored learning is who we are, we respond to any threat to that learning with survival behavior. This survival behavior is often a coping behavior, representing one or two behaviors that are left over from childhood that most effectively reduce the tension caused by threatening events. Such behavior is often unconscious and can interfere with relationships. They present childish behavior that is unattractive in adults. Bullying, tantrums, blaming and denial are examples. Minimizing such behavior is essential for building caring relationships.

In addition to the response to threat, is our response to pleasure. Events that elicit pleasure prompt us to seek repetition of those events. One such class of events is recognition. Recognition elicits release of dopamine that excites the pleasure centers of our brain. This particular type of event is typical in learning situations where repetition is critical in memory formation. The more we repeat the same information, the stronger the information pathway becomes. Recognition by a friend is the same. Any successful accomplishment has a similar result.

There is a constant flow of events that result in small jots of dopamine exciting the pleasure centers of our brain. I wonder if such incidents impact the mind with import greater than just confirmation of our particular identity. The mind has the ability to create any internal reality that we are willing to make the effort and time for. Each time we perceive a threat or pleasure we both acknowledge the event and make a response. Suppose the mind is also saying, "Notice me. See what I can do for you." Suppose that we mostly go through life as a minimalist, responding in trivial ways when we could use our mind to rise to a higher plane of being. What would it take to make this transition?

Life is not really that complex. Perhaps we need only to find our real self. It seems that there are only four requirements: 1) something to be passionate about, 2) the freedom to choose and express that something, 3) an environment supportive to that something, and 4) people with whom to share that something. We might begin by finding something to be passionate about. This would most likely be a reflection of our real self. If you could find your real self, people would come to share your radiance. It seems a tragedy that we can pass through life completely unaware of the opportunity we each have for such a life. It would seem that in addition to building caring relationships, we should be sellers of passion.

CHAPTER XLI

RESCUING GOD

If we believe in a benevolent God, we would expect that the dogma and tradition of our religion would be consistent with that benevolence. We would expect that 'benevolent' would mean that God's intent is in the best interest of humanity's survival and evolution toward a desirable and loving conjunction with God's purpose for creation.

If we believe that God is the creator, we would expect that God's creation would be congruent with the dogma and tradition of our religion. We would expect that the words and message of the *Bible* would be consistent with our experience of God's creation.

The fundamental problem with these God ideas is that it is humanity who gets to be the conduit for the transmission of these thoughts. For the above ideas to be true, humanity would need to experience with the body of God and think with the mind of God. For religion to have validity, dogma and tradition must mirror the ideas of God. For all of this to happen, religion must make the benevolence of God and the creation of God believable in the experience of its membership.

Evolution is continuously changing both man and environment. Added to that fundamental problem is that the dogma and traditions of religion must accommodate this fact of our creation, the continuity of change. Any individual, or group of people, represents a complex living system. Systems survive or die based on their ability to adapt to their environment. This suggests that the ideas of religion must be timeless and culture independent. There must be a clear distinction between the ideas of God and Man's ideas about God.

We begin with the problem of describing the indescribable. We believe what is believable. We acknowledge that our infinite God exists in a world different from ours. We must in some way describe our infinite, other worldly God as believable. One way is to personify God. Make him a father figure, God. Make God man and yet not man, Jesus. Acknowledge the created as imperfect: *Old Testament* God. Make man accessible to God: *New Testament* Jesus. Reconcile the imperfection of man with the benevolence of God.

We get into trouble immediately when we try to reconcile the imperfection of man with biblical teaching. We get into trouble immediately when we try to reconcile the creation, the way the world works, with biblical teaching. The *Bible* teaches that it all started with Adam and Eve becoming self-aware by disobeying God. The dynamic then becomes good parent, bad child. Innocence is good; knowledge is bad. God is good; man is bad. Heaven is good; the world is bad. To be good (acceptable to God), we must escape the world. Nature becomes evil. The struggle begins with man in an evil world attempting to move from self-awareness to self-transcendence. This struggle comes full circle with Jesus and his second commandment, the building of loving relationships, a thousand years of man's evolving history written in the *Bible*.

The *Bible* speaks clearly about the sinful nature of humanity. From the current perspective of creation and particularly of our mind and our learning process, nearly all of our problems are the result of illogical, self-defeating behavior, mainly control psychology. That is, that my truth conveys to me the obligation to implant that truth into others by any means necessary. The response to such a taking away of instinctive freedom and choice is a survival response. Forced to survive in a life filled with negative events, we learn that the world is unsafe. We learn survival behavior. It is this mind-set that was present during the centuries of biblical interpretation. Expectations have been realized.

Is illogical, self-defeating behavior sinful? The *Bible* says that any action that separates us from God is sinful. The *Bible* also says that such actions occurring naturally are forgivable, and that the unnatural sins are not forgivable. Those unnatural sins are said to be actions that intentionally lead the children of God away from God. Thus, we see that God is aware that nature is imperfect in that it can act in opposition to his intent.

The Bible presents humanity as powerless to avoid the sinful deceptions of Satan. It is only Jesus' relationship with God that allows humanity to escape the eternal fire of Satan's residence. We are drawn again into the dynamic of opposites. If there is a creator God, there must be a hell fire Satan, the Devil, the Deceiver. Man is shown as genetically damaged, the seeds of the father infecting his offspring and into future generations. Is this the act of a vengeful God, or the natural result of evolution, God's creation tool? Where is the benevolence?

If the diversity of evolution leads to a natural distribution of behavior from good to bad, perhaps change from bad to good is a possibility. With a positive religious outlook, humanity can help itself to change without being the personification of evil. Fear is a powerful motivator. Love is also a powerful motivator. As we become more aware of how the world works, much of our fear becomes unsupportable. Fear, like love, is learned. Both are responses to environmental conditions. Fear is unsustainable in a loving environment. In a fearful environment, love becomes heroic. It is not a new idea that love (good) is perfected through the presence of evil (bad). This is not a win-lose type of game, but rather a maturing process.

Life, evolution, diversity, distributions, freedom, choice, relationship, context, systems, complexity are all attributes of creation. They are summarized as the way the world works. The nature of things, systems, and processes support a self-organizing, self-maintaining and self-healing universe. There are both convergence and chance in being. There are no guarantees. Constant change supports complexity. Complexity requires periods of stasis and even periods of devolution. Inequality is the result of diversity, forcing the requirement for balance in all things. This is the landscape of creation. This is the residence of religion. It is the nearest we will ever get to God, at least in this life.

For religion and God to survive in this environment, religion must open itself to the way the mind works. It is in the context of belief that religion operates and has identity. It is in the context of Mind that man comes to believe and has identity. Mind and religion must be congruent. The challenge of religion is to make the unbelievable believable. It is through believers that others come to believe. The future of humanity relies on loving relationships, not on an artifact of evolution, survival behavior.

God has been lost in much of our current way of being. It is through humanity that God is expressed in our world. With our survival behavior we find it easy to express Satan: get angry, get even. How do we express love, the desire for the spiritual growth of others?

Anger is anger. Love has multiple faces. How do we sell a passion for spiritual growth?

How do we create religion as a quality image in the mind? Anger is instantaneous. Love is the commitment to the work of learning to project loving behavior. This behavior is the realization of God in our world. Rescuing God is committing to the increase of loving relationship in our world. The primary institution for that purpose is religion. Major progress requires large groups working together. That is churches. The greatest barrier to success is our tendency to stray into the self-defeating behavior of individuals, groups and even churches rather than maintaining focus on the self-enhancing goal of rescuing God. We can each of us empower God in our world through loving relationships, if we choose to do so,

CHAPTER XLII

THE BRIDEGROOM

The Bridegroom who arrives at a late hour is symbolic of the apocalypticism and eschatology of *Revelations,* an either/or psychology, 'my way or the highway'. "No one knows when Christ will come." "Be prepared." Given how the world works, and assuming that we are the creation of God, the Bridegroom has never left and has always been knocking at the door since we were born... Knocking, Knocking, waiting for his beloved to open the door. Since humanity evolved to a complexity to exhibit mind, God has been knocking. Our mind is the door. The latch is belief. The latch is on the inside, on our side. We are given the free will to lift the latch, or not.

Regardless of who or what we become, we are beloved of God, his creation. Because his creation is based on evolution, we with all of Nature are diverse. That includes our learning system and our resultant behavior. To lift the latch of belief, we think we must judge ourselves worthy of God's love. It seems that nine out of ten individuals believe themselves unworthy. You can't lift the latch until you learn to forgive, to love yourself.

To receive love, you must give love. To love is to transcend self and come into relationship with others. To give love, you must first love yourself. We resist God's love by judging ourselves unworthy. We are always judging. To be unworthy of God's love is an oxymoron.

Our existence is validation of God's love. To exist is to be faced with a flood of diverse, positive and negative experiences. Our life's meaning is in the choices, the decisions we make, and like everything else in Nature, our opportunities are anything but equal. Like it or not, without pain and stress, there is no growth, either physically or spiritually. It's the way the world works.

We live with a diversity of unequal opportunity. If God is creator, then he is aware that his creation is diverse... not equal... life-enhancing and life- defeating. If we perceive that God is judgmental, our response will be survival behavior, anger, separation. Certainly, this is not consistent with the purpose of a creator God. We should perceive his unconditional love. We are each given strengths and weaknesses according to the events we experience. I do not believe that God judges us. It is unnecessary. We judge ourselves. If so, then it should be in the context of hardships endured and as a healing process, not as some eternal punishment. This is not a call for a process of purification through some form of self-flagellation. Purification, emptying, is the work of eliminating self-defeating behavior. We make a best effort. We are each as individual and as different as our experiences and the resultant decisions that we have made. God knows this better than we do.

In all this we must realize that God's creation tools, evolution, diversity, natural selection, accomplish his purpose, but are not perfect in our experience of them. God is a God of purpose, not of perfection. Some think that God created pain to purify our souls. Must God's creation necessarily be perfect for us? I prefer to believe that God chose the best of what was available to him to work his purpose. It is not for us to second guess God's choices. We do not have a God-view that allows second guessing. The opportunity for existence with all its diversity is better than no existence.

As a loving God, he suffers our self-defeating behavior, our pain, our confusion as we do. His response to us is communication through Jesus of unconditional love and forgiveness. He does not give forgiveness, we already have it. He offers to share our life experience with no strings attached. We have freedom and choice. Abandon the past. Live in the present. Lift the latch!

CHAPTER XLIII

Upside Down?

By now, it should be clear that I believe that there are two sides to my view of religion. The question is, "Which side is up"? Is there a down side and an up side? Are you born in sin and either saved through Jesus or cast out? Or, are you the beloved child of God and taken in with a healing embrace? The first suggests that you are planted as a seed and either bare fruit or are gathered up and torched as weeds. The second suggests that you are God's creation with the possibility of fulfilling God's purpose. That process is the best possible choice for a creation process. It is acknowledged by humanity and accepted by God as having less than perfect application. He accepts responsibility and adds the means for healing to address the problem. Jesus is that healing process.

We are God's beloved children. Can a benevolent father god turn his back on the less than perfect product of his less than perfect creation process? I believe that the primitive ideas of the agrarian society of the 1st Century are expressed in the Jewish and Christian religion of that time. They spoke with the language of understanding of that period. Those ideas create images that are in conflict in the 21st century world. This conflict is in part the cause of loss in traditional Christian membership in our modern world.

We are born into a diverse world. Our magnificent brain evolved mind. With mind comes both self-enhancing and self-defeating behaviors, a result of the diverse events in our lives. We have become aware that self-enhancing behavior is largely related to positive experiences and that self-defeating behavior to negative experiences. Self-defeating behavior limits loving relationships, in opposition to God's purpose. It seems that the mind requires the nurture of loving experiences to build its strong healthy identity. It seems that to be right side up with God, we need to take away fear and confusion, and offer a healing embrace. Forgiveness implies judgment, a man-idea. I believe that we are born forgiven. We are the created, the beloved. We need to do the work of learning to accept it. With acceptance comes the empowerment to do God's work.

EPILOGUE

I DON'T LIVE HERE ANYMORE

I am an entity, the accumulation of past learning. Since my learning has been acquired over a lifetime, my past learning is a distribution from way past to recent past. Therefore, the utility of my learning, my identity, who I am, is functional in relationship to the social and technical state of the environment in which I reside. In turn, the requirements of my environment are a distribution of the social and technical needs that define my relevance. My sense of well being and my success in my culture is defined by the gap between who I am and the needs of my environment.

Evolution is a natural process of change, normally associated with genetic change over long periods of time. It is evolution and natural selection that over time results in the increasing complexity of living organisms. We can measure this time at about 3.8 billion years, from prokaryotes, the ancestors of bacteria, to the present day with its incredibly complex human brain. Evolution provides the diversity of options from which nature selects the most likely to survive. The ideas of freedom and choice are presented in the process of evolution, and become instinctive at the level of the human brain and mind.

The human mind has evolved over a period of 450 million years, primarily as our primitive or animal brain. All sensory input is wired directly into this limbic brain, and is the seat of our fight/flight process, and our source of anger, our strongest emotion. Our logical, creative brain, the cerebrum has evolved over the last 30 million years and is the seat of our logic, feelings of compassion and empathy. It is not surprising that in life's balancing act, anger wins easily over compassion. All of our yearnings and dreams of a compassionate world take the form of a hoped for convergence of our evolution with a god-purpose. Yet, given our behavior, this seems an unimaginably long time away.

When we look at our universe of 40 quadrillion stars, in 170 million galaxies we get a glimpse of the awesome nature of creation. When we look at our sun and planet, we see that a giant red star like Aries makes our sun seem like a grain of sand. When we look at earth compared with our sun, we are a mustard seed. This should make us feel hopelessly inadequate. How can we be thinking about gods and the cosmos from this point of view? It seems that our planet is situated in a comfort zone, essential for life. Our air and water have concentrations of elements that are essential for life. We are a living planet that confounds statisticians in its very existence. Above all this, we have evolved humanity whose brain is the most complex living system in the known universe. We have evolved brain and mind to the level to be uniquely self-aware and with the ability to create inner spiritual worlds. We think about the possibility of a Creator God, but also about the possibility of an unintended consequence of a complex natural system.

Just as trees are living agents in a complex living system, the forest, we individuals are living agents in systems and systems within systems: body, family, community, corporation, State, Nation. A living system is an organism acting as a whole, whose stability results from webs of relationships. Living systems self-organize in stratified layers of systems within systems. All living systems live according to the same set of system rules. Evolution has created diversity throughout nature's systems while requiring all living systems to live by the same system rules. Can you imagine a god that creates a universe with living creatures that have all the requirements for success in their particular environment? They are self- organizing and self-correcting. Can you imagine receiving the gift of life with a human brain that contains all the requirements that you will ever need for a successful life? Well, it seems that some of us cannot imagine it. Others need an instruction manual.

Unfortunately, as agents in complex living systems, our skills and abilities are not always able to provide success. We are in hierarchies of complex systems, layer upon layer. We represent the webs of relationships. We are the information carriers that stabilize systems. While we can fail in our position, the structures of the greater systems that we are in relation to are less likely to fail due to their greater numbers of agents and sub-systems. We get caught up in the blame game, but in enterprise systems, failure of an agent in a system is not a system failure. The best performance by an agent can't save a failing system if its webs of relationships get rigid and clogged. Communication is life to a system. A common system phrase is, "success has many mothers; failure has only one." The point is, you cannot let a system failure become yours. There is too much complexity for that. Failure can be an opportunity for renewal. Life is about efficiently handling problems, not about avoiding them.

Major systems have the problem of being lead by aggressive people. The phrase used to be, "lean and mean." Compassion is not a high priority. Leadership positions tend to attract controlling personalities. Control psychology is based on the right of an individual to confer his or her truths on others by whatever means necessary. The boss has the right to make all the decisions. It comes with the job. It used to be said that with the exception of a mortgage, you should purchase only what you have the money to pay for. This is an unhealthy view for financial businesses that make their money making loans. Their answer is to find ways to make the loan look like it is affordable. So, we have a mortgage crisis. Unfortunately, it is a fact of nature that individuals within a system sacrifice the system to their own survival needs. The sad result flows downward through the system. Failure at a high system level becomes starvation and death at low system levels. Distancing that supports denial is a characteristic of large systems.

Banks gave us the great depression by entering the brokerage business. The Government passed the Glass-Segal act to prevent such future banking crises. The banks lobbied with large amounts of money to remove it. The banks gave us the savings and loan crisis. They followed this with a hedge fund crisis, and a dotcom IPO crisis. Now, we are recovering from the derivative crisis that involved turning mortgages into derivatives of indeterminable value and risk. This was supported by insuring the uninsurable. "The Fiscal Cliff" has arrived in timely fashion at the peak of our latest bull market. These crises have grown step by step until their impact has become Global. Still, there is no corrective action from the Government. The Government agents have grown to an unsustainable level supported by income from lobbies. It can no longer be called a Government of, by and for the people. The end result is that every five years or so there will be a major financial crisis that reverses economic growth. To the agents lower in the system, the result is reduced income, loss of savings, and loss of jobs. This is our normal cyclical process. Free market capitalists love exponential growth. Nature hates it, but manages to punish the wrong people.

The primary requisite of any system, individual or corporate, is its own survival. In normal times, the system's focus is profit and growth. Successful systems learn to adapt to economic cycles by carrying sufficient assets to adapt to normal change. What happens when the financial world turns upside down? That is, it has a major extinction event. One that goes way beyond normal cycles, creating an environment so different that it leaves every system and agent stuck in their past learning. The environment has radically changed and there is no way back. The response is negation (It never happened), then denial (Not me!). The energy expended in looking for 'the way it used to be' dies down with the whimper, "This is not where I live." Looking for blame runs its course and finally the pain is high enough to consider the possibility with adapting to the new environment. This involves moving the mind from the past to the present.

The problem of this sort of extinction event is that those who cause the event are generally unaffected by it. Bankers and government organizations don't deal with physical product. They deal in documents that they themselves set value to. Because they are pushing paper only they and the Government are involved in corrections. What these crises create is uncertainty. This is what causes economic contractions. When technology is changing every 3-5 years, those caught in the down cycle of the crisis find themselves obsolete within a couple of years. Colleges now say that any course work over five years old is not applicable toward a degree.

We speak of retraining as a solution, but the jobs easiest to train for are the easiest of automate or send off shore. We emphasize the work ethic and loyalty of the aging population. The brain's best years for learning begin their decline by age 26. It is easier to rehire than retrain and there are lots of applicants. The net result of these crises is that the banks are too big to fail and are helped by Government to get even bigger by consolidation. Government gets larger, claiming that they need to build more protection for the general public, but do so by reducing freedom and choice.

That's right; we don't live here anymore, and we will repeat this feeling every 10 years, the likely period of company association today. At this pace, tomorrow it will be every 5 years. What we see coming are temp agencies that offer employees jobs by project or task time. This trend is currently being fuelled by the cost of healthcare, cost of insurance, and cost of Government regulation (paperwork). In this new environment, managers will be de-emphasized, becoming consultants. Paperwork will be automated. Where labor is intensive, jobs will be down graded to the lowest level. We tell ourselves that we will be the technology leaders, but our children can't afford college and our best technical schools are over half filled with foreign students.

Welcome to your new future. With the information flood supporting exponential growth in technology, our time to adapt is growing exponentially shorter. Yet, adapt we must. Given our incredible brain and mind we have the potential to create and make real (realize) whatever is required of us. We need the motivation of hope for change. This is the sort of environment that creates religions. We will find that a strong, positive belief system is essential in adapting to this strange new world.

www.ingramcontent.com/pod-product-compliance
Ingram Content Group UK Ltd.
Pitfield, Milton Keynes, MK11 3LW, UK
UKHW022226230426
12048UKWH00016BA/1097